GEORGIAN CLASSICS

ECONOMIC DOCTRINES

THE ORIGINS

GEORGIAN CLASSICS

Additional books and e-books in this series can be found on Nova's website under the Series tab.

ECONOMIC ISSUES, PROBLEMS AND PERSPECTIVES

Additional books and e-books in this series can be found on Nova's website under the Series tab.

GEORGIAN CLASSICS

ECONOMIC DOCTRINES

THE ORIGINS

AVTANDIL SILAGADZE
TAMAR ATANELISHVILI
AND
NODAR SILAGADZE

nova
science publishers
New York

Library of Congress Cataloging-in-Publication Data

Names: Silagagze, Avtandil, 1954- author.
Title: Economic doctrines: the origins / Avtandil Silagadze (Iv. javakhishvilli Tbilisi State University, Tbilisi, Georgia), Tamar Atanelishvili and Nodar Silagadze.
Description: Hauppauge, New York: Nova Science Publishers, Inc., [2019] |
Series: Georgian classics | Includes bibliographical references.
Identifiers: LCCN 2019015232 (print) | LCCN 2019017885 (ebook) | ISBN
9781536153767 () | ISBN 9781536153750 (softcover)
Subjects: LCSH: Economics--History. | Economics--Philosophy--History.
Classification: LCC HB75 (ebook) | LCC HB75 .S4989 2019 (print) | DDC 330.01--dc23
LC record available at https://lccn.loc.gov/2019015232

Published by Nova Science Publishers, Inc. † New York

Professor Avtandil Silagadze's book is very important for the better understanding of the development of economic science. The field has a rich history and the book provides interesting findings about its historical development. Georgia's input in the economic thought of the medieval period is also discussed in the book.

Dr. Professor Vladimer Papava
Faculty of Economics and Business,
Ivane Javakhishvili Tbilisi State University;
Academician of the Georgian National
Academy of Science,
Tbilisi, Georgia

Scientific book of the famous Professor of Economics, Doctor of Economics sciences of Ivane Javakhishvili Tbilisi is a preliminary study of economics. The book will be of interest not only to specialists, but also to awide circle of readers interested in these issues."

Dr. Professor Igor B. Arefyev
Full member of the International Academy
of Information Technologies of the United Nations,
the Academy of Geopolitics and Security,
and the International Academy of Transport.
Professor - Senator of the Polish Maritime Academy, Poland

In the scientific work of the doctor of economic sciences of Iv. Javakhishvili Tbilisi State University Professor Avtandil Silagadze "Economic Doctrines: The Origins" presented a peculiar study of the history of economic thinking, which formed the basis of economic science and doctrine, originally studied in individual countries (Egypt, Iraq, China, India, Ancient countries, Cyprus, Algeria, Western Europe, Tunisia, Ukraine, Russia, Georgia) The book will be interesting to scholars, students and a wide circle of readers interested in these problems.

Dr. Professor Krasimir Markov
Bulgarian Academy of Sciences, IM, Faculty Member;
President, ITHEA
(Institute of Information Theories and Applications
FOI ITHEA), Sofia, Bulgaria

CONTENTS

PREFACE

This book presents research in the old era about the individual elements of economic doctrines that form the basis of the formation of economic science. The aim of the first chapter is to consider the most important economic views (State economic function, budget model, statistics, ownership, etc.) in the ancient epoch (Egypt, Iraq, China, India, etc.). The second chapter deals with the most prominent economic considerations (economics, labor division, money, goods, property, management, etc.) of the famous representatives of the ancient epoch (Ancient Greece, Old Rome), although they did not specifically research economic issues (especially in ancient Greece). The third chapter reveals "mature" economic considerations formed in Western Europe, Kievan Rus', Georgia, Russia, Tunisia, etc.) that have finally laid the foundation for economics as a science.

ACKNOWLEDGMENTS

Thank you to Dr. Tamaz Zubiashvili (TSU, Associate Professor) and Dr. Zurab Munjishvili (TSU) for editing and correcting the monograph of the book.

.

INTRODUCTION

Economic science emerged as a result of long-term economic development. People of different professions were participating in it. For a long time, hit's individual elements were formed, those have established the new science.The term "Economics, which was created in ancient times, was not meant to create economic science at the same time.

How did the process evolve?

It is known that the social system based on slavery emerged in the 4th-3rd millennium BC and it existed up to 3-5 century AD. It was based on Private Property. The slavery first emerged as the result of the disintegration of the primitive temporary lifestyle in Asia and Africa and reached the highest level of development in antiquity countries.

In the slave-era, it is possible to use a wide range of labor divisions. This made the basis for economic growth of individual countries. The characteristics of this era were reflected in the economic views of that period. At this time, the goal was to protect the society in general, but "anti-genius" ideas was created.

In the old Eastern countries, the peasant community was long-lasting, the importance of the State to economic life was important, namely: Irrigation constructions, control over economic resources, expansion of land and others. It is noteworthy that the economic thinking of this period has evolved in the process of acute resistance.

The new, more developed economic relations were established in the later era, which also had a peculiar reflection on some new economic thoughts in a separate country.

In the present work, researches of economic science are examined. The thinkers of this epoch prepared a solid foundation for the development of economics. Their ideas do not lose their sensitivity even further. So, we tried to present a complex problem from modern positions. For this purpose, we have used a number of scientific works in the present work, including:

1. The "Course of Lectures"[1]; read by Robbins in London School of Economics, in which a separate head is considered to "form the system of economic opinion". We took into consideration some of the author's approach, particularly with Plato, Aristotle, and Thomas Aquinas. In addition, some of his opinions, such as Zh. Boden, Mercantilism (Malin, Misten, Mani), U Pete, we did not share about J. Locke because mercantilism was not the previous stage but the first doctrine of economic development of society that played an important role in the development of the economic science system;
2. In the work of famous scientist Blaug[2], a brief introduction to the previous history of economic science was devoted. Mercantilistic and physiocratic (chapter 1), A. Smith (chapter 2), D. Ricardo (chapter 4) and others. The minds are extensively discussed.

---

[1] Robins, Lionel. (2000). *A History of Economic Thought: The LSE Lectures*. Edited by Steven G. Medema and Warren J. Samuels, Princeton University Press.

[2] Blaug, Mark (1997). *Economic theory in retrospec*t (5th Ed.). Cambridge New York: Cambridge University Press.

3. In Heinz D. Kurz's book[3], only a few pages were devoted to Babylonian, Ancient (Plato, Aristotle), Analysis of Scholastic Economic Opinion (chapter 1). At the same time, the author devoted a more extensive and interesting analysis of mercantilistic, classical (chapter 2). Doctrine analysis;
4. In the work of Eric Roll[4], The formation of economic thoughts, the most profound analysis of Plato and Aristotle's views is mainly demonstrated. We have adopted such an approach, but we have discussed a broader range of issues:
   (i) Agnar Sandmo's book[5] provides a brief and interesting history of economic science origin. It is not concentrated on the opinions of the ancient epoch. The author begins a deep discussion of the problem with analysis of Adam Smith's views;
   (ii) In the paper published by *Steven G. Medema and Warren J. Samuels*[6], our research problem is basically (briefly) limited by some aspects of the ancient Greek and Thomas Aquinas economic thoughts. More extensive analysis has been conducted in relation to other issues;
   (iii) After a brief overview of the prehistory of Economic Science in Hunt and Lautzenheiser work[7] (Chapter 1) there are discussed in detail economic views of Adam Smith (Chapter 2-3), Thomas Robert Malthus (Chapter 4), David Ricardo (Chapter 5) and others;

---

[3] Heinz D. Kurz. (2013). *Geschichte des ökonomischen Denkens*. München [*History of economic thinking*. Munich]

[4] Eric, Roll. (1992). *The History of Economic Thought*. (5th Ed.). London.

[5] Agnar, Sandmo. (2011). *Economics Evolving: A History of Economic Thought*. Oslo/by Princeton Un-ty Pres.

[6] Steven G. Medema (Editor), Warren J. Samuels (Editor). (2013). *The History of Economic Thought*. Second edition Published 2013 by Routledge.

[7] Hunt, E. K., Lautzenheiser, M. (2011). *History of Economic Thought*, 3rd Edition: A Critical Perspective. Sharpe, N.Y.

(iv) In the first chapter of Famous Professor V. Avtonomov's Book[8] (PP. 12-27) is interestingly discussed economic thoughts of the pre-capitalist epochs: Specifically, the views of "Economy", "Economics and Chermatistics", "Fair Price",

(v) In the book of Professor A. Silagadze, T. Atanelishvili, N. Silagadze, the studying problem[9] is shown extensively.

(vi) Different works[10] of A. Silagadze, T. Atanelishvili are dedicated to various aspects of studying problems. In particular, there[11] are analyzed economic views of the ancient world, Shota Rustaveli and "Beka agbugha" and others.

Thus, in comparison to other works, in the above study, we developed a more profound, complex and modernized assessment of the research, including on the example of Georgia. (The work is based on the works of the Authors, famous scientific, as well as on the Internet materials).For the creation of economic science and economic doctrines it is still (and not only) actual to review economic opinions expressed in the early epoch. The work does not lose the actuality even in the future, even though based on the views discussed in it, individual assessments may be modernized. In addition, and we have observed the fact that the formation process of economic science and doctrine was completed by mercantilists and classicals, which is the subject of our future research.

---

[8].Avtonomov, V., et al. (2002). *Istoria Economicheskich Uchenii* [*History of Economics Doctrines*]. Moskow. (In Russian).

[9] Silagadze, A., Atanelishvili,T., Silagadze, N. (2010). *Economic Doctrines*. Georgian National Academy of Sciences. Tbilisi.

[10] Silagadze, A., Atanelishvili, T. (2010). *Aspects of Economic Doctrines in Georgia*. San Francisco;

[11] Atanelishvili,T. , Silagadze, A. (2018). Formation of Economic Views in the Ancient Era. *Bulletin of the Georgian National Academy of Sciences*, vol. 12, no.2, pp.191-196; H Silagadze, A. (2018). Some Aspects of Economic Ideas in Shota Rustaveli's "The Knight in the Panther Skin". *Bulletin of the Georgian National Academy of Sciences*, vol. 12, no. 1, pp.161-167; Silagadze, A. (2017). History of Georgian Economic Thought: Relation between the Center and the Region. *Bulletin of the Georgian National Academy of Sciences*, vol. 11, no. 4, pp. 138-144.

Chapter 1

ANCIENT ECONOMIC IDEAS

In the ancient epoch, in the period of the disintegration of the primitive temples and the emergence of slavery, naturally, economic thinking emerged in the process of acute resistance. At this time, the exploitation of the slaves was a normal event, and in the old Eastern countries the rural areas of the country were long-lasting. In addition, the role played by the state in economic life was of great importance, The following events were conducted under its leadership: Irrigation constructions, control over economic resources, expansion of state landowning. In this era the farming was mostly natural, but the livelihood of the goods-money was still in the way that broke up the natural farming framework.

The peculiarities of such processes have been reflected in the economic thinking of individual figures. The views expressed in the period are about the individual elements of the economy are of great importance for future developed economics and doctrines. Let's consider some of them.

1. EGYPT

The first samples of economic thinking are found in the countries originating in the Tigris and Euphrates basin (about 4,000 years ago) and in Egypt (3,000 years ago). One of the oldest among the economic "monuments" to date is in Egypt - about in the 22nd century BC, "The Instruction of Khete to Merikare"[12]. The parts of the"Instruction" text are stored in Cairo (French Institute of Oriental Archeology), Copenhagen University and Russia (St. Petersburg-State Hermitage, Moscow-Art Institute).

Under the "Instructions"[13]: The deep knowledge of State governance "Rules" is essential for the manager; Particularly important is an effective functioning of the State management apparatus, the material encouragement of the warriors, officials, to present them land plots; The basis to hire an individual at the State management apparatus should be knowledge and not origin; It is necessary to care for the compatriots and the borders of the country; The poor are not to be invited in the army-they will betray; You should distinguish young people not with their origin, but their talents, knowledge, and deeds. Increase the stock supplies of bread and so forth.

In the "Instructions" is also raised in the foreground: Economic functions of the State; Importance of effective management of lands; The necessity of maintaining economic structures in the King's Palace; Protection of property of rich ones by the State. The problem of the maintenance of the land to the family inherited by his father; The issue of youth employment in the State apparatus, in the regular army, the rise of the people's property and so forth.[14]

Thus, one of the oldest among the economic "Monuments" to date is Egyptian "The Instruction of Khete to Merikare", in which the

---

[12] *The Instruction of Merikare.* http://www.reshafim.org.il/ad/egypt/merikare_ papyrus.htm 24/ 08/2018.

[13] Ibid.

[14] Atanelishvili, T., Silagadze, A. (2018) Formation of Economic Views in the Ancient Era. *Bull. Georg. Natl. Acad. Sci.,* vol. 12, no. 2, pp. 192-196.

following topical issues emerged: Deep knowledge of the "Governing" rules (not origin); Effective functioning of the State management apparatus, material encouragement of the warriors and officials; To care for compatriots and the borders of the country; Increase of bread stock; Economic functions of the State; Effective management of lands; Necessity of economic structures in the King's Palace; Protection of property of rich ones by the State;The problem of the maintenance of the land to the family inherited by his father; The issue of employment of young people in the State apparatus, as well as in the regular army – distinguished ones to be awarded with the land.

2. SUMERIANS: CODE OF UR-NAMMU

Sumerians are the oldest civilization in Mesopotamia (BC 6-3 millennia). Ur-Nammu, from the third dynasty of Ur, reigned in the BC 2112-2094. The Sumeri nation, which created the Sumerian civilization - irrigation, writing ... lived in South Mesopotamia. After Ur-Nammu the king became his son Shulgi . The Code of Ur-Nammu[15] is written in Sumerian language, BC Approx. 2010-2050 years (Stored in Istanbul Archaeological Museum). Some believes that the preface of the "Code" is written by King Ur-Nammu (2112-2095 BC), other claims that the author is the king's son, Shulgi.

The "Code" was discovered by the Archaeological Expedition of the University of Pennsylvania in 1899-1900. In c. Nipuri (South Mesopotamia) in the introductory part issues about the army, taxes and, etc. are approved. Economic issues are defined as: 1) Agricultural land lease and lease liability; 2) Contract for the work to be performed and the remuneration of the hired workers; Money and bread Loan Agreements; Sales and housing terms and so on.[16]

---

[15] Claus, W. (2002). *Der Kodex Urnamma (CU): Versuch einer Rekonstruktion* [*The Code Urnamma (CU): Attempt to Reconstruct*].

[16] *Ibid.*

Thus, the Ur-Nammu Code approves military and tax reforms, lease of land and lease accountability, hired labor, borrowing of money and bread, identifying conditions for selling products and housing, etc.

3. IRAQ

3.1. The Laws of Eshnunna

The laws of Eshnunna[17] (20-19-19 BC) were discovered in Iraq during archaeological excavations in 1945-47. It is written in Old Babylon (Akkadian) Language. These laws are also referred to as "The laws of King Bilalam." (Ehsun's King in the 20th century BC). "Laws consist of 61 articles. It is kept in Baghdad museum.

According to the laws[18] of Ashnunna have been established:

- Rules of slaveholder and trade relations; Means of payment for goods - silver (Article 1);
- Volume of compensation and fines for hired people (Article 5-11);
- Participation in the trade of slaves, and their underage children were forbidden to take loans;
- Transfer tariffs for ships (Article: 3-4);
- Loan obligations (Article 19-24);
- Double compensation for the kidnapping of someone else's slave (Article 49);
- Cash compensation for physical damage (Article: 42-48);
- Death penalty for committing serious offense (Article 58) and others.

---

[17] Reuven Yaron (1988). *The laws of Eshnunna, Brill. Second Revised Edition.*

[18] Ibid.

Thus, the following are defined by the laws of Eshnunna: rules of regulating trade and borrowing, means to pay for trading, shipment tariffs, money fines for human damage, death penalty for committing a serious crime, and so on.

3.2. Babylon: "Code of Hammurabi"

Babylon ("The Gate of Gods") was the capital of Mesopotamia (region Tigros and Euphrates), whose ruins remained in Iraq until recently. It was founded approx. At the beginning of the third millennium BC. According to historical sources, in the 23rd century BC, Babylon became a holy city.

The collection of laws[19] of the king of Babylon Hammurabi (1792-1750 BC) (discovered in 1901, the archaeological expedition of France in Szcze) is the peak of the old East economic thinking. "The code of laws" is a peculiar reaction to the slaveholding regime. It consists of[20]: the introduction, the main part (Article 282) and the conclusion.

According to King Hammurabi's order, the "Code" was exposed on the stone to stay unchanged. The "Code" protects the eternal ownership of property, justifies slavery and makes slaves equal to the slavery. It is divided into the following parts:[21]

1. General principles of Law (Article: 1-5);
2. Protection of the king, temples, community and property free people (Article 6-25);
3. Norms of state property (Article: 26-41);
4. Real-estate operations (Article: 42-87);
5. Trade Operations (Article: 88-126);

[19] *The Code of Hammurabi Translated* by L. W. King general-intelligence.com/library/hr.pdf 24.09.2018.
[20] Ibid.
[21] Ibid.

6. Family and Heritage Law (Article: 127-134);
7. Physical damage (Article: 195-214);
8. Operations related to movable property and its hiring process (Article: 215-282).

Furthermore, in regard to the economic and other norms defined in the Code[22], it may be noted that: it states that if an individual is accused of murder by another one, but can not prove the accusation, the offender will be punished with death (Article 1); But if one approve the accusation he must be rewarded with money; If the judge's decision is later erroneous, he must pay more than twelve times than the defendant and the judge's right should be permanently lost. (Article 5).

In addition, the "Code" also prescribes[23]:

- Death penalty for saving a runaway slave: "If someone hides a slave of the palace or mushkenu in his home and does not hand it over to Nigaru's request, he must be put to death" (Article 16);
- Two slips of silver to find, catch and return a runaway: If someone catches a slave who escaped in the field and leads him to his master, the owner must give him two slips of silver. " (Article 17);
- If anyone is caught in theft, he must be punished for death (Article 22; 2);
- If the owner will give his gardener to a gardener and the gardener will perform the service honestly for four years, the owner must be involved in gardening service in the fifth year; If the gardener fails to do his job fairly, it should cover the loss of a year according to the neighboring crops (Article 42);

---

[22] Ibid.

[23] Ibid.

- If a slave tells his master - you are not my master, then the master can cut an ear to the slave (Article 282) ...

In the Code "one of the sources of slavery is a debt obligation: In case of non-payment the creditor has the right to have debtor as a slave or some member of his family. We should pay attention to the part of the Hammurabi laws, which takes into account protection of the debtor's after three years of debt obligation: If someone has a debt and can not pay, then his spouse, son and daughter must work with the debt for three years and the fourth year they shall be released (Article 117).

Hammurabi's law code protects large landholders. As it turns out, at that time the lands were divided as follows: Lands transferred to the forced farmers the king and the lands assigned to the king's servants. The "Code" emphasis is made on the latter: the creditor could not overtake 6 to 15 hectares transferred to warriors and it could not be buying or selling subjects. If the captured warrior had no money to repay the plots of land, then the amount would be paid by the community or the palace. Such land plots would have been inherited only if the son of the soldier would be in military service, but if he was underage, his mother would have to fulfill her husband' obligations. (Article 29). Also, by the law, the King's servants could purchase lands: Is it really possible to take away the field? Make the issue clear! It is noted in the letter, sent to one of the civil servant by Hammurabi.

The "Laws"[24] approve the procedure of Land Leasing and determines the Lease Amount - in the processing of gardens by 2/3 of the crop (Article 64). In addition, if the yield was reduced because of the gardener's fault, he was still obliged to pay the lease to secure a stable income for the owner(Article 65).

According to the Article 48 of the Code of Law[25], the debtor was free from taxes, if the plight of the land was caused by a natural

[24] Ibid.

[25] Ibid.

disaster: If anybody has the loan with a benefit, and the Raman goes out to his field, or the flood will take the harvest, or drought will not be able to harvest the bread in the field, or the floods will be harvested, or because of drought it won't be able to harvest the grain in the field, then it is not obliged return bread. This is a proof of what the significance of the "rural insurance system" was introduced.

In the natural environment of Mesopotamia, without irrigation, land revenue can not be realized. The owner of water and irrigation system was the King who was paid by the community for water use. In addition, a member of the community should take part in construction of irrigation facilities, it means he had a bilateral obligation before the community and the king. This was a characteristic feature of the ancient Babylonian epoch that was naturally reflected in the Hammurabi laws.

It is also permitted under the "laws"[26] to use the hired labor, and the norm of the payer's salary is established. At the time, the hired laborer, who was yearly paid with (the number of working days was about 20 days a month), 6-7 slips of silver, was to increase to 10-11;Trade (including slavery) is a normal phenomenon. At the time of the Babylonian Market, one of the most important centers of trade, the function of payment was mainly performed by silver; Also, according to the "Laws" loan interest rate is 20%, it is allowed to sell the slave pay a debt; If someone hits other with the rank higher, then it must have 60 rattan publicly; If any person hits to person who owns the same rank, then he must pay one gold; If the person hits someone with a lower rank, then the victim shall impose the same damage to him;If the builder was unable to build well and the building would be destroyed, the builder was put to death and if the son of the owner would die during the collapse of the building, then the son of the builder was sentenced to death;If someone will destroy the wall of the house and rob it, he will be built in the wall as a penalty. If a child tries to hit his/her mother, they cut his/her hands so on.

---

[26] Ibid.

Hammurabi Laws thus promotes a broader development of human rights, clear distinction of human rights, development of goods and monetary relations, property, lease, loan and interest rate, hired labor, labor payments, money, taxes, etc. Existence, which was of great importance for the development of economic science and doctrines.

4. China

It is known that Chinese civilization started about 5,000 years ago with the formation of city-states and China came under a big "center" about 2,000 years ago. The role[27] of the Confucian ideology was great in the management of that state. Economic thinking in China has reached a very high level of development. Here in the I millennium BC, the main sector of the economy was agriculture, at the same time they produced porcelain, gunpowder, paper, iron weapon, developed silkworm husbandry and goods-cash relations. These processes have a significant impact on the development of Chinese economic opinion. China is also referred to as a homeland of many interesting economic ideas.

4.1. Confucius

In the 4th and 3rd centuries BC, there was a confusion between the separate schools of economic thought in old China. Its ideological founder is Confucius or Kongzi (about 551-479 BC). Confucius, who was a high-profile representative. After his death, his opinions - in

[27] *China: Five Thousand Years of History and Civilization*. City University of Hong Kong Press, 2007.

conversations – were published by his students as a separate collection of "Lun-Yu"[28] ("Talks and Discussions").

Confucius's advice on state governance is issues still actuality. In his opinion, it is necessary to use the expenditure saving and the use of human resources during the country's management. It is unacceptable to participate in such events where the wine[29] is drenched in the ground; If fair people are invited to manage the country, people will trust you, otherwise they will be on the contrary;[30] You should not travel in a volatile, unstable country. If the state is ruled correctly, then poverty is a shame and if the state is managed wrongly, the accumulation of wealth is a shame.[31]

On the one hand, Confucius defended the interests of the privileged classes of the society and on the other hand propagated the restoration of old, patriarchal and commonalty relations. He was not against slavery and demanded that every person had its own functions in society: the king must be as a king, the Father- as a Father, the Son – as a son.[32]

Confucius defended slave ownership, and for the first time developed the doctrine of "natural rights" in China, according to which God is the only creator of the universe, but it does not interfere in the social life that is protected by civil laws. It was considered naturally to divide people into workers of the mentally and physically labor, and it was claimed by God and nature. In addition, the country should have enough food, weapons and confidence[33] in the state.

At that time the local population was exploited by the state through taxes and labor relations. Therefore, the old Chinese economic thinking was aimed at regulating these issues by trying to preserve the natural

---

[28] *The Analects. Sayings of Confucius.* Translated By D.C. Lau. https://antilogicalism.files. wordpress. com/2017/07/ the-analects.pdf

[29] Ibid: 1:5; 3:10.

[30] Ibid, 2:19.

[31] Ibid, 12:11.

[32] Ibid, 12:11

[33] Ibid, 17:7.

economy. In this regard, some of Confucius's remarks went beyond their epoch and gave way to the development of livestock farming. We mean in his own words: Here is one precious stone, sell it or wait for it when we get a good price for it? His answer is: sell it, sell it.[34]This means that it is better to sell the immovable thing then keep it, and earn income, which is a means of continuing new activities.

Confucious favors the accumulation of wealth honestly, but not the amount that would harm people. In his view, it is better to be economist[35] then embezzler and therefore requires moderate protection in consumption, fair distribution of wealth and distinguishes between group and private property. It is true that he connected the private property to the country's contradictions, but ultimately gave him the advantage. In his opinion, if you can get riches, you may be a cabby. If it is not possible then you have to turn your path.[36] The wealth that is dishonestly acquired is like the cloudy sky.[37]

Confucius believes that state governance should rely on human moral perfection; The state is a big family where he must control costs and care for people; Head of state is the father of the people; The state should take care of the peace between the high and low classes of society, the development of agriculture, the reduction of taxes, equity distribution, the ruler should not waste money and he should love people.[38]

Overall, Confucius was a prominent figure in the transition period of the old China, on whose contradictory opinions, dissolution of current communal life style and emergence of slaveholding system has an impact.

Confucius doctrine has had a significant impact on the economic life of China and East Asia. It became a pillar of confucianists. The ideal for confucianists is the existence of a harmonious society where

---

[34] Ibid, 9:12.
[35] Ibid, 7:35.
[36] Ibid, 7:13.
[37] Ibid, 7:17.
[38] Ibid, 7:35.

all its functions are fulfilled. Let's recall Confucius's words: What you don't want done to yourself, do not do to others!

Confucianism has an impact on state, including Mao Zedong and Deng Xiaoping's governance policy. The idea of confucionists was especially popular on the issue of regulating the manager-subordinate relationship: Do not treat people as you do not want to be, and then peace will come[39] in the country and in the family as well. At the same time, there was no lack of criticism, including in Europe.

Overall, Confucius's economic views can be summarized as follows:

- Defended the interests of the privileged classes of the public and propagated the old patriarchal-commonal relations, where the "natural rights" of the lower classes were protected;
- For the first time developed doctrine of"natural rights" in China, according to which God is the only creator of the universe, but it does not interfere in the social life that is protected by civil laws. It was considered naturally for him to divide people into workers of the mentally and physically labor;
- Condemned exploiting of local population by the state with taxes and labor relations and demanded their regulation in the conditions of maintenance of natural resources;
- His is for accumulating wealth honestly and demanded moderate protection in use, he distinguished Collective and Private Property; Connect the private property to the country's contradictions, but ultimately it has given him the advantage;
- Considering that state governance should be based on the moral perfection of human beings; The state as a large family must control costs and care for people; The head of state is the father of people; The state should take care of the preservation of peace between the higher and lower classes of society, the

[39] Ibid, 12:2.

development of agriculture, the reduction of taxes, the equity distribution of wealth.

Overall, Confucian was a prominent figure in the transition period of the old Chinese, on whose contradictory opinions, dissolution of current communal life style and emergence of slaveholding system has an impact, although its ideas have had a significant impact on the economic life of China and East Asia.

4.2. Mengzi

Confucius's views further subsequently influenced the ideas[40] of one of its main followers-Confucian, the ancient Chinese philosopher Mencius (Chinese 孟子; 372-289 years BC, knows also as Mengzi).

Mengzi was a student of Confucius's grandson, who, according to influencing Chinese culture, is considered as the main figure after Confucius. Mengzi lived and was working in one of the socially unbalanced state of China, in the socially disorganized state - "Qi". In its basic letters the moral norms of conflicts are generalized - humanity, justice, customs and wisdom. Special attention was paid to humility and justice.

The main contribution of Mengzi in Chinese philosophy is to discuss human "Good Nature"[41]. According to him, the person is kind one from the beginning and if you make him/her to commit it imposes evil, it means that the influence of nature against it is forced. On the basis of these principles, he supports: To satisfy the "Fair" demand of the people masses; To revive traditional production relations; Protection of the "Natural Rights" between public classes; Active interference of the state in the economy; Moderate taxes; Development of goods

[40] *Mengzi.* Chinese text with Legge's English translation https://ctext.org/mengzi
[41] Ibid.

exchange between landlords and craftsmen; The prohibition of fixed prices, the obligation of the human ruler to take care of his brilliant people, because the ruler can't be happy with the wealth, if the mass of the impoverished people threatens him to kill.[42]

Mengzi had not yet a perfect conception on structure of the Chinese society. He supports social division of labor and justifies the division of people according to mental and physical labor, in which he saw "the universal basis of equality". In addition, the Mengzi faced the difficult situation of people and demanded to reduce the taxes imposed on them. Description of the property differentiation: The rich and the noblemen have the kitchen filled with fat meat, the stout horses, and the human being are tired of hard work in the end the dead bodies of those killed by famines in the fields are thrown.[43]

According to the Mengzi's Agrarian Project, one part of the land should be cultivated jointly and the harvest be grant to the public officials. He regularly considered the existence of a special class of people who could only be involved in the state management. Besides, he divided merchants into two classes: domestic and foreign ones. In his opinion, the idea was that the lower classes of the population had to aliment the prevailing classes. And for this purpose - demanded revival of the old communal production. According to his view, there are separate activities for high and low classes: one is working mentally and others - physically.[44]

There is some contradictions in the views of the man. For example, he supports a wide range of labor but, on the one hand, considers farming and crafting incompatible,n the other hand, the exchange of goods between them is considered normal. When discussing these issues, Mangzi has made a very strong point of view: The same size and qualities of shoes will be sold at the same price.[45]

---

[42] Ibid, Chapter, 1:2.
[43] Ibid, Chapter, 2:12.
[44] Ibid, Chapter, 5: 3-4.
[45] Ibid, 5:4.

Communal illusions are characteristic of the Mengzi's economic views: on the one hand, defending the economic interests of the common and of peasants affected by slavery and on the other hand, state violence is unacceptable for him. Consequently, he was given a special role to slaveholding states in the reduction of peasants' exploitation. In his opinion, the state should be moderate while gathering taxes in order to prevent farmers from interfere in cultivation of his land. Consequently, he recommends the reduction of taxes.[46]

Thus, Mengzi's contribution is: to be divided by the mental and physical labor of people ("universal law of equality");Generalization of the moral norms such as humanism, justice, custom, wisdom and the "good nature" of human beings;Protecting the "natural rights" between classes on the basis of revival of traditional production relations, the demand for active involvement of the state in the economy, moderate taxes, development of the goods exchange between landlords and craftsmen, prohibition of fixed prices.[47]

In general, conservative contradictions are typical for early confucianists; Mengzi is for division of labor, the parallel development of farming and craftsmanship seems to be incompatible for him and fights for development of goods exchange, communal illusions and granting a special role to slaveholding state in reduction of the peasant's exploitation are characteristic for him.

4.3. Guanzi

In *Guanzi*, economic issues are mostly discussed in chapters: 48,69, 73-75. These include the state governance of the economy, socio-economic development, regulation of market processes, commodity-money relations, etc. Issues. In particular, according to Guanzi:

---

[46] Ibid, Chapter: 1:1.5; 13:23.

[47] Ibid, Chapter, 5:4.

- The country's ruler with a potential must create good conditions for life and then manage; The rich are good to manage and poor people - hard; Countries which don't produce food will disappear; [48]
- It is necessary to deepen the rules of agricultural production and timely clearance in price policy;High and artificially reduced prices on foreign products are unacceptable and In order to influence them, national financial control mechanisms should be activated;[49]
- If the country has food supply enough for ten years, golden supplies, sea and others resources, it should be used for people not to live poorly. If human interest economic interests coincide with national interests, then they will stand beside the king and the country will be stronger. Wheat is an important product and the state must control its prices[50];
- The National Statistical Office of Property Management should calculate the land fund and the population, settlements and socio-economic development of the country as a whole; It is important to know the management of financial statistics, the number of land and population, the price of wheat, the strength of money, the volume of money in circulation, the daily supply of food products, etc.[51]
- Non-payment of taxes contradicts national financial interests. However, the statistical service should prove the methods of efficient management of taxes and natural resources.[52]

According to Gracchus: Market "Barometer" of economic condition; If the ruler regulates the issue of bread and money, then the

---

[48] *Guanzi.* Chinese text with matching English vocabulary. Chapter, 48:1-2. http://chinesenotes.com/guanzi.html

[49] Ibid, Chapter, 69:1-2.

[50] Ibid, Chapter, 74:2-9.

[51] Ibid, Chapter, 74:2-9.

[52] Ibid, Chapter: 75:1-2, 5-6, 8.

country will be stable. The same goal is to promote farming and to build the state warehouses.

The fact that the state has to effectively manage the land must know its quality - productivity, taxation of justice and for this purpose elaborate mechanisms always is an actual issue. In this approach, we are actually dealing with the requirement of land cadastre, which is of great importance in the formation of economic sciences and doctrines.

Guanz was in the center of special attention of the public in the first century BC. At this time China was an agricultural country. As noted, the statistical materials are used in the treatise. It can be said that "Guanzi" is one of the first statistical monuments in the world economic literature. Obviously, without analyzing statistical data, modern problems can not be solved.

According to the Treaty: Price is a market regulator that can influence farming and the price stance is an important source of economic well-being of the country; Bringing the bread in the country causes the golden undesirable withdrawal from the country; The active interference of the state in economy, stable prices and reduction of tax rates are necessary.

Guanzi's authors also considered the creation of grain stock as very important thing, which should be distributed in deficit conditions: Additional supplies should be created when the prices are low, and it should be sold while prices are high, the treasury must be filled with the profit.

The regulation of the production of monetary resources also captures the attention of the tract: in the case of bread surplus, money should be purchased by excess products to avoid falling prices; In the conditions of bread deficit and price rise, the state should have a cash loan to give to the population in order to purchase of bread. Such approaches were some of the novelties in the history of economic thinking. In particular, we were dealing with one of the first attempt to create micro/macro-economic models of regulating prices on the products, growth of treasury income.

The treatise is designed to regulate prices throughout the country, which should limit the control of merchants and speculators. As it turns out, in China, there were widespread public taxes that were condemned and it is recommended to change it with indirect taxes. Increase of taxes on salts, metal products, and so on is considered as the best way to increase the treasury.

In a simple commodity production, it is considered that the price increase for commodities devaluates money. It is also characterized by classes of scientists, peasants, merchants and artisans. Their hard and productive labor activities are describes. It is true that the "Guanzi" is not against merchants and lenders, but they are mentioned with a less sympathetic, requiring restrictions on their rights and protection of their peasants from their exploitation.

The authors of "Guanzi" consider the development of the main source of agriculture as the main basis of the country's development. Encouragement of this field is associated with the country's material strength. According to their "agrarian project" lands should be taxed according to their productivity. It distinguishes different categories of land: one part gives the possibility to productively use 1% of the land, the second - 1/10 and the third - 1/1/5. Because of the fact, that each equal area could not provide equitable productivity, the authors of "Guanzi" introduced a taxable rate, where they considered the natural conditions of land.

The authors of the treatise assign craftsmanship and trade accessory role, but it is important that they do not oppose its development.

Thus, according to Guanzi:

1. The range of progress and resistance in the economic thinking of old China (and not only) has revealed;
2. The state regulation of the economy is discussed: the socio-economic development of the period, especially the issues of management of market processes, including goods and monetary relations;

3. It is possible to determine the economic situation of the country using market and prices;
4. Stable prices are named as an important source of economic well-being in the country;
5. The state should be actively involved in the economy and regulate the issues of bread and money circulation, support the development of farming, building of warehouses, the land fund. As already mentioned, the latter actually meant the land cadastre demand, which was the novelty;
6. It is considered: Creation of bread supply by the state and it's distribution in the conditions of deficiency; Mobilization of additional supplies in the presence of low prices; At high prices - selling stockpiles and thus increase treasury income; Regulation of production through money; In case of bread deficit and price increases, to issue state loans for the population to purchase bread. As it was mentioned, such a demand meant regulation of prices on products through money circulation, the very first and important attempt to create micro/macro-economic models to increase the treasury.
7. It is recommended to create a special Statistical Institution and to use a wide range of statistical materials in the analysis and in this regard we deal with one of the first "statistical monuments" in the world economic literature;
8. Importing of wheat in the country result in selling more gold and it is necessary to regulate prices throughout the country - establish stable prices, replace direct taxes with indirect taxes, increase salaries on salts, iron products;
9. Some of the regularities of functioning of monetary farming are analyzed in the simple commodity production. For example, it is established that the increase in commodity prices leads to impairment of money;

10. The classes of scientists, peasants, merchants and craftsmen are described. The peasantry referred to with some sympathy - describes their hard productive labor activity;
11. The existence of merchants and entrepreneurs is permissible, but they are referred to with less sympathetic, requiring restrictions on their rights and protection of peasants with their exploitation. In addition, craftsmanship and trade are regarded as unproductive activities, such an approach is caused because an epoch;
12. Farming is indicated as the main condition of the country's progress. With their "Agrarian Project", lands should be taxed differently - according to their productivity and others.

4.4. Taoism

In ancient China, doctrine about Tao took an important place (Taoism). Taosism (approx. 6 - 5 cc) is a blend of religion and philosophy. Founder of it is a thinker of Confucius era – Laozi (6th-5th bc), author of the work "Tao de Ching" (the book about the way and of virtue"). Tao de Ching laid the foundation for the religious and philosophical process of China –Taoism,[53] which at the initial stage was only a philosophical course, but in the 2nd Century, it became a religion that has been also referred to as - Taoism. Zhuang Zhou (known as Zhuangzi) (BC 4-3c.). The doctrine of the Taoism contradicts with Confucianism, because the latter served the interests of the governor and the society: Who ever obeys me: does not go to the war, he is quiet person and is in a shadow.

Whoever doesn't obey me: He is going to the fights is and the army is a source of disaster.[54]

---

[53] *Laozi (1983). Dao de Zini.* Tbilisi. (In Georgian).
[54] Ibid, p.108.

Laozi is a very important figure of world philosophical thinking. He condemns wealth, luxury, nobility, and violence against the rulers and war. The cause of the poverty of the people is seen in high taxes and against the accumulation of great wealth; Requests to abolish excessive restrictive laws. "Do not glorify the precious things: and creep shall be cut off among men"-wrote Laozi.[55]

According to Laozi: Social Idea is a primitive common, where property is available for everyone; When falsehoods will be destroyed: great calmness will be everywhere. Oh, what's the difference: between yes and no, and what is the difference between the good and the evil,[56] despite the unfairness of the man, the man must adapt to the fate of life ("be silence and subdue nature, silence will form the consent of the world").[57]

Thus, Laoze condemned the accumulation of great wealth (rare items make a man unhappy),[58] the ruler's violence and wars, the causes of the massive poverty of the people he linked to high taxes and demanded to abolish excessive restrictive laws; His ideal is the primitive common, but despite the unfairness of injustice, the person must adapt to the fate - must obey the flow of life; The ideas of Taoism were utopian and hindering factor for civilization.

5. India: The Laws of Manu and Arthashastra

In the 6-5c. BC, large slaveholding states were established in India. The country's governance has been the reason for writing the written documents here. One of these is 'The letters of Manu'[59]

Drawn up in the 2nd century BC.

---

[55] Ibid, p.88.
[56] Ibid, p. 99.
[57] Ibid, p.102.
[58] Ibid, p.93.
[59] *The Laws of Manus*. Translation by G. Bühler. Oxford. At the Clarendon Press.1886. https://ia800501. us.archive.org/28/items/lawsofman00manu/lawsofman00manu.pdf

The laws of Manu. The society of the millennium of Indian state of India is somewhat characterized in the "Laws of Manu". (The first translator of Manu's Laws in English is William Jones, 1746-1794).

It features the peculiarities of the social structure of the old Indian society. The "treat" is written in the form of dialogue where Manu describes the world and the four social classes. The "Laws" consists of 12 chapters:[60]

Chapter 1. Origins of the universe classes;
Chapter 2. Lifestyle in the process of learning;
Chapter 3. The life-style of the family resident;
Chapter 4. About Brahman's lifestyle;
Chapter 5. Lifestyle, Women's Obligation;
Chapter 6. Ascetic Lifestyle;
Chapter 7. Instructions for King's Obligations and State Management;
Chapter 8. Instructions for Legal Procedures and Legal Practices;
Chapter 9. Liabilities of spouses;
Chapter 10. Obligations of classes (caste);
Chapter 11. Suggestions for repentance of sins;
Chapter 12. Description of the post-death life for the bad behavior committed in real life.

In the Code the social structure of the society implies division of different classes (castes). According to the laws, the supreme god Brahman has created a different caste of parts of his body. There are four categories of caste - Brahmin, Kshatriya, Vaishya, Shudra and each function[61] in the society are defined.

Brahmins are granted the Supreme Authority and it is not accidental in their old Indian literature, are referred to as gods. At the next step is Kshatriya Caste, which was obliged to protect the country; Vaishya caste was involved in farming, cattle breeding, trade, and shopping. Functions of the Fourth Caste - Schudra are equal to the functions of slaves without property. According to the law, superiors are Brahmin, Kshatriya, and Vaishya. They are confronted with the united front of

[60] Ibid.
[61] Ibid, Chapter, 1:31.

Shudra caste, the main duty of which is only physical labor and the service of the previous three castes. The different ways to turn into a slave are: from the birth, purchase, present, inheritance, punished and, etc.[62]

According to the laws, "Fair Governance" defines the state governments by an educated king. A large part of the spoil (land, weapon, orro-silver) extracted during wars was transferred to the king's ownership, and the rest of the property was distributed by the warriors. The army inside the country also served as an order protection officers. The king could set taxes, but in moderation. The king also appointed high-ranking officials.[63] The court obeyed the king. However, the functions of the court were established: property, marriage, heritage, etc. Discuss issues. There was a witness institution too.[64]

According to the established rule, if someone owns property for ten years, it will remain in the possession of the owner. This rule did not cover the mortgage. There are seven ways of property acquisition: heredity, extraction, presence, charity, donation, purchase, job fulfillment, usury. Dealing with cheating was considered invalid. Hired labor, which could not be fulfil obligation in deadline was prohibited. Moreover, he was not paid for an unbanned work due to illness.[65]

Different ways of marrying in India are defined (marriage: by adopting big property, bull or cow, on the basis of the words given by her father, also to buy a spouse, volunteering, to steal spouse and, etc.). Marriage of underage persons and the second wife (if the first one is not appropriate), also marriage of spouses with different religion were not forbidden (but they were not encouraged). Also, the sale of wife and children was not forbidden.[66]

---

[62] Ibid, Chapter, 8.
[63] Ibid, Chapter, 7.
[64] Ibid, Chapter, 8.
[65] Ibid.
[66] Ibid, Chapter, 9.

The kill of Brahman was punished with the law, (death penalty, cutting of hands, cutting of language, castration ...) Alcoholism, theft and other serious offences. Some convicts were expelled from the country after confiscation of property. The murderer was free from the punishment, that protected the Brahmans and women from attack. As an exception, Brahmins were not sentenced to death and they used other measures of punishment.[67]

Thus, in the laws of Manu are established: the social structure of Indian community and the function of each class; The concept of "Fair Governance", which implies state management by an educated king; Model of her Ship Distribution obtained during wars; Regulatory Norms of Property Relations; Types of remuneration of the Hired Workers; Family Commitment; penalty forms and, etc.

Arthashastra. The important economic monument of ancient India is "Artashastra" (Arthaśāstra) - the treatise on state policy and management – (4-3 cc. BC). Its principal founder is recognized the famous scientist and public figure, the chief minister of the King Chandragupta, Kautilya (BC 4thc.). Until the 12th century, Arthasstra's ideas were often used, till its disappear. In 1905 it was again discovered by Indian scientist R. Shamasastry (Rudrapatna Shamasastry, 1868-1944). He published this treatise in English for the first time in 1915.[68]

The treatise requires an active interference of state in the old Indian economy. In it it is a system of division of society into castes, but with fear of public revolt, the author requires a careful attitude towards the slaves. In particular, the slaves should have the right to have a small property and family.

"Arthashastra" consists of 15 books, which are divided into separate parts and chapters.[69]

---

[67] Ibid.

[68] *Kautilya's Arthashastra.* Translated into English by R. Shamasastry. https://archive.org/stream/ArthasastraEnglish_Translation/Arthashastra_of_Chanakya_-_English#page/n7/mode/2up

[69] Ibid.

Content:

Book 1. “Concerning Discipline”;
Book 2.”The Duties of Government Superintendents”;
Book 3. “Concerning Law”;
Book 4. “The Removal of Thorns”;
Book 5. “The Conduct of Courtiers”;
Book 6. “The Source of Sovereign States”
Book 7. “The End of the Six-Fold Policy”
Book 8. “Concerning Vices and Calamities”;
Book 9. “The Work of an Invader”;
Book 10. “Relating to War”;
Book 11. “The Conduct of Corporations”;
Book 12. “Concerning a Powerful Enemy”;
Book 13. “Strategic Means to Capture a Fortress”;
Book 14. “Secret Means”;
Book 15. “The Plan of a Treatise”.

“*Arthashastra*” recognizes the following science: philosophy, the doctrine of economics, the doctrine of state management and the doctrine of ancient Indian knowledge.

It deals with: economic relations between the employer and the employee, the partners, the buyer and the seller;[70] Doctrine on farming, breeding, trade as the doctrine on economics;[71] Strict punishment for crimes against merchants and craftsmen; King’s support in development of agricultural and natural resources, gold and precious stones’ mines, factories, livestock, seafaring, in case of droughts or other natural disasters; Issues of assistance in case of hunger, epidemics, natural disaster, in aspect of law, medicine, social welfare, economics (markets and trade, agriculture, breeding, mining and forestry activities, employers and employers’ relationships). Strict sanctions for economic hurdle for hindering welfare (conspiracy against traders and craftsmen); Use of forest resources in favor of the country; Active involvement of the state in development of miners and factories, gold and other precious metals commodities, forestry products,

[70] Ibid, Book, 3.
[71] Ibid, Book, 1:4.

weapons warehouses, agriculture - livestock, plant growing, marine traffic, defensive system. The possibility of transfer of lands to private ownership, if their owners paid the tax; Sanctions for non-cultivation of transferred land (initially 12 coins (pen) penalty, and if continued the same to lose the right on the land plot);It was the king's obligation to promote the expansion of territories, the construction of the irrigation system, the promotion of farming, livestock and horticulture development...

Considering financial problems is worth paying attention:

- Head of the financial department should be the main collector of income;
- State Budget revenues are named: income from the state farm, monetary taxes, etc.
- In the state budget are listed expenses for development of the industry, trade, etc.
- Accumulating the treasury in the state treasury and strict control of the state's income-expenditure is of great importance.

The tract also deals with the participation of the king in the trade, and the export of its goods must ensure the profit. Prior to engaging in trade, the king had to study the existing conjuncture on the market. Such demand means the actuality of learning marketing principles.

According to the treatise, the basis for determining the price of commodities is the number of days worked. The author advised the king to take appropriate measures to maintain a stable price on the market. However, such an approach is contrary to the principles of free pricing, but at that time their approach was very important for the development of the basis of economic science.

Thus, Arthashastra is approved: Active Interference of the Economy, system of division of Society into Castes, creation of a Small Property for the slaves and creation of a family, creating an effective system of problems in hunger, epidemics, natural disaster, establish strict sanctions against hindering factors of human welfare, deployment of forest resources in the country's service, irrigation constructions, extraction and recycling of precious metals, creation of arms warehouses, marine navigation networks, distribution of the lands to the private ownership, with the condition of payment of taxes, The State Budget's Income-Exemption Model, the king's involvement in the trading of the market based on conjuncture preliminary study, Strict Control of the State's Income, To use the number of days worked as a basis for determining prices for commodities, maintaining solid market prices on the market and so forth. Consequently, it is clear that in ancient Indian literature, the analysis of the problems of the Goods-Monetary Relationship became more profound.

Chapter 2

ANTIQUE ECONOMIC THOUGHTS

Because of its special contribution to the European civilization, antique countries (Latin Antichaeus - ancient) was called to Ancient Greece and Ancient Rome. The term "Antique" was first introduced in the scientific turnover in the 18th century. The ancient era includes more than 12 centuries (BC 8th - 5^{th}AD). During this period especially developed: philosophy, astronomy, mathematics, medicine, and even individual elements of economics (Plato and Aristotle "Schools"); Christianity originated; Polis (City-State); Developed sea marine; The first great empire was created (by Alexander III the Macedon), also the Roman Empire; Founded the state banks, treasuries and, etc.[1]

Acute problems of the slave-holding epoch has been reflected in antique economic thinking. It is true that the real events of the epoch are not exactly explained in such thinking, but in such approaches the scientific explanation of the economic events has been observed.

The contribution of ancient civilization in the history of economic thinking is great. In this period the Financial-Credit Relationships were strengthened and the solid foundation was prepared for the establishment of economic science - the term "Economics" appeared.

---

[1] Kiknadze, Z. *Antique epoch.* https://www.nbg.gov.ge/uploads/leqsikoni.pdf

The economic thinking of the ancient epoch is characterized by: the advantages of labor division, the advantages of natural farming; Justification of slavery; Discussion of various mechanisms for management of slave farms; Start discussing property, property-related relationships, etc.

It is not accidental that economic thinking has reached a special level of development in the works of non-economist thinkers of ancient Greece and Old Rome. All this due to the highest level of development of slave holding relations. As noted, the economic thinking of this period is mainly covered by the slave-like natural farming framework. However, after the development of goods and monetary relations, the situation has changed.

The Greek thinkers were discussing the "economics" within the framework of the polis (state). At this time there was no economic science and special economic direction. However, the study of individual problems in this period provided a solid basis for the formation of both science and economic doctrines in the future.

1. Old Greece

Ancient Greek economic thinking discussed issues of socio-economic reforms quite interestingly, mainly in the framework of slave holding. Because of this, research on goods and monetary relations was on the other side. Nevertheless, Greek thinkers have made remarkable success in researching economic issues such as: labor division, property, money, goods and many others.

The highest level of ancient Greek economic thinking was demonstrated in the views of Xenophon, Plato and Aristotle.

1.1. Xenophon: "Oeconomicus", "Income" and "Division of Labor"

Xenophon (approximately 431-354 BC.) is one of the main representatives of the ancient Greek economic thinking: He was a historian, philosopher, ideologist of slave holders and a student of famous Socrates. He participated in the Peloponnesian War (431-404 BC) and became a major landowner.

The political views of Xenophon are contradictory to "slave democracy". His work with economic contents is: "Oeconomicus", "Cyropaedia", "Revenue of c. Athens"... In addition, he, as Socrates' student, wrote the work" Memories of Socrates", where more attention is paid to Socrates' personality than his philosophy.

"Economics". The name of the Xenophon's work is "Economics" - "Oeconomicus" (Old Greek Οἰκονομικός from old Greek - οίκος- name and νομος– law, ad verbum: The main rules of agriculture). In the form of a dialogue, the author's economic views are set out. It was translated into Latin by Cicero.

The work consists of 21 Chapters:[2]

Chapter 1. The essence of the economy;
Chapter 2. Importance of Science of Economics. Socrates' wealth and Poverty in Critobulus. Critobulus desire to study this science;
Chapter 3. Bad and Good "Economics";
Chapter 4. Employment in the ranks, military operations and farming;
Chapter 5. About farmers;
Chapter 6. General Conclusions;
Chapter 7. Introduction of Iskhomakhi by Socrates. Iskhomakhi's Wife. The aim of marriage; The duties of the spouse;
Chapter 8. Family Amenities;
Chapter 9. Arrangement of Housing. Key-saver. The role of housewife;
Chapter 10. Outgrow of spouse from cosmetics and body recovery with a care for "economy";
Chapter 11. Activity of Iskhomaki;
Chapter 12. The ruler. Its selection and preparation;

---

[2] *The economist by Xenophon Translation* by H. G. Dakyns. TTP://WWW.GUTENBERG.ORG/FILES/1173/1173-H/1173-H.HTM

Chapter 13. The features of the Manager;
Chapter 14. Laws for honesty in the service;
Chapter 15. The necessity of studying agriculture;
Chapter 16. Soil and its processing;
Chapter 17. Sowing;
Chapter 18. Take the harvest and clean the grain;
Chapter 19. Gardening;
Chapter 20. Attentive and careless farmers;
Chapter 21. Knowledge of addressing people.

Based on the contents of the work, the first part mainly deals with family farming, and another part is about agriculture. The first one of the thesis begins with this:[3] once I heard Socrates about family farming and I want to ask you a question Kritobul- Is leading of the family the name of any science like as medicine and so on? The answer: Yes, then what is the subject of a science? The answer: like medicine and so on? Answer: Yes. What is the subject of this science? Answer: It is a good farmer's business to manage economics well!

According to Xenophon, all the wealth in human ownership, which can be utilized represents a part of farming; Management of farming is an important science,[4] from which people enrich their farming, and farming is a property, each kind of property is useful for his life, and everything which is used by people is useful; Money is useless if the owner can not use it;[5] Separate real and fraudulent money from each other.[6]

The main areas of Xenophon is agriculture, and craftsmanship is considered to be harmful activity for humans[7] (constantly sitting in one place). The rich people are also engaged in farming and this activity provides benefits - food. If you are riding a horse and protect the

[3] Ibid, Chapter 1.
[4] Ibid.
[5] Ibid, Chapter, 6.
[6] Ibid, Chapter, 19.
[7] Ibid, Chapter, 4.

homeland, the land gives the horse food; The landowners guard their lands with a gun to protect the wheat produced by them.[8]

Xenophon has been giving recommendations for efficient management of slave farming. For this purpose, he indicates in "Oeconomicus" that the economy must be properly managed, otherwise the economy becomes disadvantageous. The following words belong to him: Agriculture is the mother and feeder of all professions.

According to Xenophon, craftsmanship is an inappropriate activity for a free man,[9] and slavery is a normal phenomenon; This means that a free citizen must be able to perform the function of the supervisor in the field of agriculture, and the slave must work physically. In order to encourage slave productivity, he demands for material encouragement among the distinguished slaves.

As we see, Xenophon firstly used the term"economics" in the work "oeconomicus, which meant the art of managing household management, based on slavery; He firstly mentioned the consumer and exchange values of goods - land, animals, etc. It is not valuable for them, who can not use it; The useless property becomes beneficial when selling it: Those who are able to play on the flute, it is worthy for him, but whoever can not play, only after selling will become it valuable. In this discussion, the basis for the modern meaning of the essence of goods was founded.

Thus, Xenophon: firstly used the term "economics", which implies the art of managing household based on the slave working. He was the first who mentioned the consumer and exchange values of goods;He underlining the land, animals, etc. is not valuable for those who can not use them; The useless property for the owner is beneficial by selling it (thereby basically laid down the modern definition of goods);

[8] Ibid, Chapter, 5

[9] Ibid, Chapter, 1-2.

Agriculture named as the the main field, the craftsmanship is considered to be harmfu activity for humans (constantly sitting in one place). For the profitability of the economy he demanded to manage it properly; He discussed the issues of rational management of the economy; Well life is considered as possible when you spend the whole income not at one time, but if you spend it time by time; Xenophon also demanded remuneration for the work done; To be possible getting additional income by cultivation the land purchased by the public and, etc.

Xenophon on Income. The small composition "Revenue of c. Athens"[10] was written by Xenophon. In 355 B.C. It provides tips to overcome the acute deficit of revenues in the state of Athens. In the opinion of the author, in the effective management of the state financial resources, it is possible to cover the expenses unevenly. For this, peace is needed when taxes are no longer a burden to the population. He also gave special importance to the use of silver deposits as a source of extra income in the country's budget.

The work consists:[11]

Chapter 1. Introduction. Nature of Attica;
Chapter 2. State protection of the Meteki;
Chapter 3. State protection of merchants and ship owners;
Chapter 4. Processing of silver deposits;
Chapter 5. Necessity of Peace;
Chapter 6. Conclusion.

In his view, excellent nature, yielding land, precious construction stone in Attic and other places will be the source[12] of additional revenue in case of effective management.

---

[10] *On Revenues Xenophon.* Translation by H. G. Dakyns http://www.hkshp.org/wclassic/xenophon-revenues.htm

[11] Ibid.

[12] Ibid, Chapter 1.

With the support of the Meteks (uninterrupted residents) (buying and selling of land, participation in elections, the right to recruit) it is also possible to mobilize[13] additional state revenues.

Xenophon named the development of trade and shipment of goods with their own ships as a source of additional income for the state. For this purpose, additional infrastructure (hotels, shopping squares) for foreigners should be created.[14] He also believes that the processing of silver deposits will bring great revenue to the country.[15]

In addition, Xenophon thinks that it a natural right of free citizens to live at the expense of state slaves' exploitation while the slaves should remain only a speaking weapon. According to his recommendation, the state of Athens should be purchased a large number of slaves and they must be tented to work in the deposits. From this it was supposed to get a big source of income: If the state purchased at least 1 200 slaves and hired them, they could buy 6,000 in 5 - 6 years and then 10 000 slaves.[16] If such processes have repeatedly manner, then citizens of the country will live in luxury and the state will receive solid revenues.

Thus, Xenophon's recommendations were some of the novelties to increase budget revenues, which included: covering expenditures in efficient management of state financial resources; In the conditions of peace, to relieve situation in connection with taxes for the population; Use of silver and other mines to mobilize additional revenues in the budget; Athens's state procurement of large quantities of slaves and renting them in the field of mines, which would bring great revenue to the country.

Division of labor. "Cyropaedia" consists of 8 books,[17] which describes the reign of Persian king Cyrus. In this work Xenophon firstly

---

[13] Ibid, Chapter 2.

[14] Ibid, Chapter, 3.

[15] Ibid, Chapter, 4.

[16] Ibid.

[17] *Cyropadia. The Education of Curus By Xenophon.* Translated By Henry Graham Dakyns. Revised By F.M. Stawell https://www.gutenberg.org/files/2085/2085-h/2085-h.htm#2H_4_0011

underlined the questions in the history of economic thinking about the importance of labor division. It is not limited to the physical and mental labor of humans and it is absolutely impossible to perform high-performance of different works.[18]

According to Xenophon, a person who conducts various types of work can not perform all the work with a high quality. In large cities, due to great demand for things, the craftsman prepares one type of item with a better quality (compared to smaller cities). In large cities it is possible to divide the labor that the craftsman can earn his keep just from one type of avocation. In small towns, due to a small request, one and the same craftsman prepares the cue, the door, the table, the spoon, etc. Of course, this craftsman will not be able to make all the item at high quality. Productivity and quality are increased when, for example, one craftsman sews men's shoes, and another woman's shoe. Xenophon is similarly concerned with the specialized food preparation.

Discussion with Xenophon, on the importance of labor division-specific and demand, without which there is no basis for economic science. Now no one argues that if a person performs many types of work simultaneously, they can not perform high quality.

Thus, Xenophon is one of the first to focus on the advantages of demand and division of labor in creating a high quality product; Not only limited to the physical and mental labor of humans and it is absolutely impossible to perform high-performance of a variety of work simultaneously.

On the whole, Xenophon has a number of significant conclusions about the economy, the division of labor, the goods, money, the state revenue and the others, the world, including the history of ancient Greek economics, perfectly captures the outstanding place.

---

[18] Book 8, Chapter, 1:5-6.

1.2. Plato: "The Ideal State"

Plato (Greek: Πλάτων - wide) (Greek: 427-347) Greek philosopher, a student of Socrates, Aristotle's teacher, ideologist of the slave holding aristocracy, was born in Athens, in an aristocratic family. His real name was Aristocles (Αριστοκλῆς). According to one of the versions, Plato was named by his wrestling teacher based on physical characteristics. He was a student of Socrates and Aristotle's teacher.[19]

Plato's works, including "State", "Laws" and so forth are presented as dialogue, where Socrates plays the role of anchor-man. Plato is considered one of the founders of the idealistic direction in philosophy. He was not particularly interested in economic issues, he was interested in state arrangement issues and created remarkable economic views in dialogues. In this regard, it is very interesting his works such as "Politeia" or "State", "Laws", etc.

"Model of the Ideal State". Plato's epoch was the epoch of new forms of social-political order, when different models of "ideal state" were created.

Plato, like Xenophon, was interested in the problem of labor division, as it found the basis of "Ideal State". In his opinion, the state is ready to form when no one can satisfy his various needs (food, clothes, or home) ... so every person appeals to others to meet his needs.[20]

According to Plato, humans are different from their birth and they have to carry out the pre-determined (Governance, Protection of the Country, Farming, Craftsmanship, etc.) duties. However, amongst the people, in order to strengthen the state, specialization is required: the land worker should not at the same time prepare a coulter, hoe or other units of agriculture, cobbler and doffler to do[21] their professional work.

---

[19] *Plato Biography*, file:///C:/Users/user/Downloads/plato-257.pdf

[20] Plato. *The State*, Translated from Old Greek by Bachana Bregvadze. Tbilisi, ''Nekeri'', 2003, p.60. (in Georgian)

[21] Ibid, p. 62.

Depending on the above, since the natural ability of the human beings is same (it may be cobbler, doffler...), but their requirement is various (food, clothing, residence place) ... Plato approves the existence of resistance between the needs of individuals and the possibility of their satisfaction, which will be gained by the city-state. Here people specialize in one of the types of labor and the productivity of labor increases as a result of labor division. However, Plato imposes a strict sanction to the craftsman, who violates the terms of negotiations with the client and must pay the customer to the full cost of the product.[22]

Plato also interestingly discusses about trade: there can not be a self-sufficient country whose citizens do not need to import goods[23] from another country. Therefore, it is also necessary for the state to have people with other profession to import goods from foreign countries. But if the case deals with maritime trade,[24] then marine is required in addition to merchants. He also requested to arrange an exchange square where demands would be satisfied. In addition, he condemned the speculative activities of the traders in such "markets" that are all day in the market, they are trying to buy cheap commodities and then try to sell it to others.[25]

Plato paid attention to the profession of warriors: martial arts requires great attention. The war is the source of great disaster, but the horde must protect our domains and join the other territories.[26]

As noted, Plato declared a labor division as the main principle of building the state and division of society into classes. In what conditions can the perfectly suited exist?In response, he created the first version of model of the "Ideal State" in the essay "State" (Greek Πολιτεία, 360 BC),[27] and the second one in the "Laws".[28]

---

[22] Ibid, pp. 60-63.
[23] Ibid.
[24] Ibid, p. 63.
[25] Ibid.
[26] Ibid, pp. 66-67.
[27] Ibid, pp. 125-162.
[28] Plato. *Laws*. http://www.perseus.tufts.edu/hopper/text?doc=Perseus:text:1999.01.0166

The "State" (as many other works of Plato, written in the form of dialogue with the participation of Socrates) represent the expression of justice: only one part of the citizens should not be happy, but all...With the growth of the state's well-being, we should allow all the classes to have some contribution in welfare of the state, according to their natural data.[29]

The state should be characterized by the following qualities: moderation, courage, wisdom and justice.

The state is fair when all layers perform their functions.[30]

Plato discusses five types of state arrangement:[31]

1. Aristocracy and Monarchy (the most acceptable form of governing small group); 2) Timocracy (relatively less fair governance of minority that changes aristocracy when personal interests are subject to public interests); 3) Oligarchy (the power of the rich); 4) Democracy (equality of rich without regarding their personal qualities) and 5) Tyranny (the most imperfect type of governance).

Plato gives preference to the "Ideal State" with the form of aristocracy: if many rulers have power over it, it will be an aristocracy... Even this is the advantage. That's the one, I give an advantage, because wheather the rullerwill be one or more, they won't violate the laws of the state.[32]

In the "Ideal State" Plato divided three layers (γένος) of free citizens according to the division of labor:

1. Higher layer: Ruler-philosopher. Until the Philosophers are not reign the state ... Neither states nor men can come out of the

---

[29] Plato. *The State*, pp.126-127.
[30] Ibid, pp. 144:146.
[31] Ibid, p.162.
[32] Ibid, p.162.

devil.[33] The philosophers should govern the state.[34] They should have occupied state positions after the age 35. They should not own private property because philosophers, they should not be mixed in a multitude of things, like others.[35]

2. Warrior's layer, aimed at protecting and expanding the state's territories. Neither of them have their own property (house, land or anything else) because they will live together and work together in gymnasiums;[36]
3. Other Citizens (Farmers, Craftsmen, Merchants)[37] who own private property. Their goal is to manage farming, state supplying, satisfying the needs of philosophers and warriors.

Slavery, equality of women and men. In the "Ideal State" layers (citizens) he does not consider slaves. Slave for Plato is a weapon of production, an ownership, and slavery - the natural, permanent form of exploitation, the biological justification of it is in the human nature itself. Plato except health in slave's spirit and in "Ideal state" killing of slave is referred to as "purified". In addition, he also observed that the slave-holding regime excited hate and fight for liberation of slavery; In order to avoid this danger, he demanded more caution in dealing with slaves. Plato's views about slavery are just one part of his socio-economic concepts, which provided objective requirement of that epoch, theoretical justification of slave-holding regime.

In addition, it's worth paying attention to Plato's views on the equality of women and men and the role of women in the "ideal state". According to him, the state builders have no grounds to assign different responsibilities because of different sex. It is true that the woman and the man have the same natural data to protect the state,[38] but this ability

---

[33] Ibid, p.196.
[34] Ibid, p.197.
[35] Ibid, p.205.
[36] Ibid, pp.175:183.
[37] Ibid, p.186.
[38] Plato. *The State*, pp.166-172.

is less pronounced in men compared to women. Nevertheless, the two sexes must choose the work independently (even in the army), which he/she wants and performs well. Therefore, Plato believes that there must be a law on military and household equality of men and women. (Such a norm currently operates in a number of countries).[39]

Thus Plato's opinion that the two sexes are equal and they can choose any activity according to their wishes, is more actual in the contemporary period.

It can be said that "ideal state" has laid the foundation for "principles of communism": the state manages socio-economic processes; The property is a common property and the rulers and warriors have no private property rights; Preaching of citizens' equality and brotherhood ideas; Division of labor according to the ability; Living together, meals and so forth.

Plato is still discussing the classes of the same society in the work "Laws": From the ancient times we have four classes based on property, they can be transferred to another class if their property is grown up.[40]

In "Laws" also focus on organizing property and settlements with 5040 citizens, absolute impoverishment, impossibility of buying and selling lands. In such a settlement, it is possible the land to be cultivated, protected, and taxed.[41]

Plato's "Laws" written in the form of a dialogue, according to some information, was published after the author's death. It consists of 12 books. In addition to this, the following issues of modeling of "Ideal State" are also discussed and clarified: General principles of legislation, civil relations, laws on the protection of private property, the permit for the creation of family for all classes, crime and punishment,

---

[39] Plato. *Laws*. book 7: 805-807.

[40] Plato. *Laws*. book: 5, 744 d. http://www.perseus.tufts.edu/hopper/text?doc=Perseus:text:1999.01.0166

[41] Ibid, book 5:737a-738 a, b; 741a-e.

mechanisms for enforcement of laws;[42] Organization of the "ideal state" and the choice of its governors; Strengthening the controlling role of the state; Number of inhabitants and management structure;[43] Punishment for religious offense, criticism of atheism;[44] Proper distribution of property and settlements with 5040 citizens, impossibility of absolute shabbiness or buying and selling of land parcels. Possibility of processing their land, protection and taxes in such settlement.[45]

Agriculture, craftsmanship, trade and money. For Plato agriculture and the existence of a natural farm are the main source, where everything must be done according to demand; The future state should rely on separation and independence in economic relations where land is the property of the "ideal state", which will be handed over to the farmer in order to cultivate in exchange for a certain fee. The words belong to him: the land is "our mother", which feeds people.

He demanded in "Laws": Implementation of the terms of renting lands received for cultivation; Acceptance of laws about limit establishment[46] of poverty and wealth; Agricultur and borders' protection, relationship of craftsmen and customers, labor division, hunting, trade (free citizens should not involved in this activity), restriction of profit, distribution of foodstuffs, ship-traffic, improvement of housing conditions, trade stadiums, etc.[47]

As noted in Plato's view: the main field of agriculture, and the land is the property of the "Ideal State" which will be handed over to the farmer for a certain fee to cultivate; The law should define the poverty and riches margin, and so on.

Plato, in comparison with farming, has given the least role of craftsmanship and trade. In his opinion, only foreigners in these fields should be employed, whose activities must be strictly monitored.

---

[42] Ibid, book: 9: 853-854; 10: 884-885; 11:913-915; 12: 960-961

[43] Ibid, book 6: 751-770.

[44] Ibid, book 10: 885-910.

[45] Ibid, book 5: 737-741; 6:771.

[46] Ibid, *Laws*. Book 5: 728-744.

[47] Ibid, book: 7: 823-824; 8: 842- 850; 9: 853-858; 11: 913-922...

Plato has emphasized a very important issue for his time, that trade makes commodities equitable. However, he did not properly understand this issue and found that various goods were made through equitable money, and therefore, the existence of money was justified.

In his opinion, private individuals must be prohibited to own gold and silver; The coin was needed in everyday exchange within the country; The other country could go only with the permission of the government, which provided the person with coins from his supplies. As soon as this person returns from abroad, he has to pay foreign money in exchange for local money. Otherwise, his money would be transferred to the treasury forcibly. He also declaimed usury -issuing of money to get benefit from it. In this case, the borrower had possibility not to pay the debt.[48]

It can be said that in Plato's "ideal state" is formed a basis for "Principles of Communism": Socio-economic processes of the state manages; Property is common property; Preaching of citizens' equality and brotherhood ideas; Work is distributed according to skill and so on.

Overall, the following comes out from Plato's views:: Labor division is the basis of "Ideal State" - where division of labor is based on demand and natural resources, which leads to exchanging and high productivity; Because the natural ability of people is same, there demands are different, there is a resistance between the needs of the individuals and the possibility of their satisfaction, which will be provided by the city-state;The demand for the gathered people will be satisfied by organizing the Exchange Square in the city; The state will be harmed from people to choose different professions simultaneously; For the breach of agreement between the customer and the craftsman, the craftsman is obliged to pay the full cost of the product in favor of the customer;Plato Separated five types of state arrangement: Aristocracy and monarchy; Timocracy; Oligarchy; Democracy; Tyranny and gave preference to aristocratism; In the "ideal state", free

[48] Ibid, book 5: 742.

citizens divided into three classes according to the division of labor. (Slaves are not considered there); In the "State" it seemed possible for Plato to eradicate riches and poverty, to increase the size of the country to the extent until it can maintain unity; He distinguished four characteristics of the "ideal state": wisdom, courage, jurisprudence and justice.

1.3. Aristotle: "The Giant of Philosophy"

Economic thinking in antiquity in Greece has reached the highest level of development in the works of the greatest thinker of the world, Aristotle, who was a student of Plato (Greek Αριστοτέλης, 384-322 BC). He has a deep trace of economic thinking. He was born in Stagira (His father-Nicomachus was a Doctor of the King of Macedonia Amyntas II). At the age of 17 he began studying At the Plato Academy in Athens, where he received a broad philosophical education. While studying in the academy, he drew Plato's attention from the very beginning - because of the deeper ability of thinking, and it was not accidental that Plato was called "brain of the academy."[49]

The student greatly appreciated his teacher, but among them there was a variety of opinions, one of Aristotle's word approves it: "I think it is possible to sacrifice even one's flesh and blood, in order to protect the truth. They are both precious for me (Plato and The truth as well), but I still prefer the truth."[50]

The letter of Philip II of Macedon (343 BC) speaks about Aristotle's great authority: The King of Macedonia salutes Aristotle! I would like to inform that I have a son. I thank the gods for not so much because they gave me a son, but rather because he was born in Aristotle's epoch. I hope your dealings will make him worthy of my

---

[49] Silagadze, A., Atanelishvili, T., Silagadze, N. (2010). *Economic Doctrines*. Georgian National Academy of Sciences. P. 39.

[50] Aristotle (2003). *Nicomachean Ethics*. Tbilisi, 1096 a.

legacy and Macedonia. Aristotle received an invitation, and during the following 2 years he played a great role in the development and education of Alexander the Great. However, in the last years of their lives, the relationship between them has been strained, especially since Aristotle's nephew, a talented young philosopher (who didn't obey Alexandre's) -Callisthenes, was put to death (327 BC) in connection with the conspiracy against him.[51]

After this unfortunate incident, Aristotle returned to Athens and founded an independent school - "Lykeion" (according to the name of the churchapollo lykeios). This school is also called "Peripatetic", where Aristotle was reading the lectures at the school yard alley. Aristotle was expelled from the city because of inculcate atheistic ideas and he died a year later.

Aristotle as an economist played an important role in shaping the basics of economic science. His contribution is important in troubleshooting of problems in connection with property, division of labor – money (its functions), demand, exchange, etc. His works are clear evidence that the theoretical basis of economic science originates in the antiquity of the epoch that has evolved over the next centuries.

Aristotle first - most accurately analyzed the socio-economic problems of that era, thus essentially he obtained the name of the "first economist" in the history of economic science. It can be said that the prehistory of economic science and doctrines are mostly discussed by Aristotle. The fact is that Aristotle was of course relied on the economic considerations of the predecessors, but in his work (unlike the predecessors) individual economic categories are made much more profoundly analyzed. Aristotle's socio-economic views are extensively established in the works: "Politics" (335-322 BC), "Rhetoric" (355 BC), "Nicomachean Ethics " (c. -322 years) and, etc.

---

[51]Aristotle (1981). *Rhetoric*. Tbilisi, University Press, pp.7-8.

1.3.1. "Politics"

Aristotle in the work "Politics"[52] (Greek Πολιτικά- state activity) considered problems of family-state, slavery, citizenship and so forth. His ultimate goal served theoretical justification for an ideal policy. The work consists of 8 books, from which the issues of economics are generally discussed in the second chapter.[53]

In "Politics" has been criticized Plato's doctrine of "ideal state". Criticism also touched upon Plato's statute on common ownership and Aristotle's privileged private property.[54] However, Aristotle partially considered the existence of common property as admissible.[55]

Aristotle is interested in a state union that will allow every citizen to live according to his/her will. Each state is a kind of union, every union is aimed at something good, because everything is done for what you think is good.[56]

Aristotle considered a family (Greek: οἰκία: Owner and slave, father and son, husband and wife) as an integral part of the state, the first union of several families created to satisfy the daily needs was called the village and the union of number of settlements was named in a state (Greek πόλις) It works for common well-being.[57]

Aristotle, based on Plato's views, allocated special science studying public relations about policy. In his opinion, people in the society should live only in the existence of a political system:

(a) Politics is a science, knowledge about how to make the best organization of human life in the state i.e., the art of state management.

---

[52] Aristotle. *Politics, part 1.* Tbilisi 1995; part 2, Tbilisi, 1996.
[53] Aristotle. *Politics, part 1:* Book 1-2.
[54] Ibid: 1261 a, 1261b.
[55] Ibid, 1263 a.
[56] Ibid: 1261 a, 1252 a.
[57] Ibid: 1260b, 1253 a, 1253 b.

(b) The goal of the policy is to create high moral forms, fair qualities i.e., to establish equality of citizens, educate the noble people.

Aristotle believes that the state is the product of natural development and the highest form of relations. Accordingly, he named the following forms of state governance:[58]

- Legal (Monarchy –one man government; aristocracy - the best hereditary - small group governance; Politeia: the political unit - the rule of majority, based on the principle of elective choice, the best form of governance);
- Illegal (tyranny; oligarchy; democracy –the rule of majority of people born as a free person and people without property) from the unlawful forms, to it has given the advantage.

Aristotle distinguished three classes in a state:[59] very rich, very poor and middle class. The latter is considered the pillar of the country, while others are dangerous: because of insolence of the rich men and exacerbation of the poor people. Such an assessment is still applicable to a situation in some transitional country, where even a strong middle class can not be formed. Such a situation seemed to be dangerous even that time, because rebellion is everywhere because of inequality, because equality can not be established between irregularities.[60] In addition, he also contradicts the principle of equalization of property in the state, because the state can not exist without the rich and the poor.[61]

Aristotle criticized the project of Hipodamus of Miletus (BC 5th century), according to which the state should have: 1) the layers of craftsmen, farmers and warriors; 2) Land for the sacred (for God's

[58] Ibid, part, 1: book 4, Chapter 2.
[59] Ibid, 1295 a.
[60] Ibid, part 2, 1301b.
[61] Ibid, 1310a.

servants), the public (the warriors) and the private lands (lands). In addition, all layers should participate in state management. According to Aristotle, in these conditions, only gun owners have been able to dominate in comparison with the rest of the state management. That is why it is better if the land is not in the ownership of the warriors, and it will be cultivated a farmer to ensure the needs of the warriors, and the craftsmen are needed for the state and they can support themselves.[62]

1.3.2. "Economics"

Aristotle first used the term economic science, which was named among the most respected sciences (rhetoric, strategy ...) under the policy.[63]

After considering the state issue, Aristotle discusses "Family Economy" (Greek Οικονομικά), which involves acquisition, use and management problems. It also consists of the same parts as the family. The property is part of the family,[64] the knowledge of acquiring property is part of economic science; Some of the weapons in the family farm are brute ones (e.g., wheel control in the vessel), some are spiritual (e.g., patrons), and the slave is a live weapon- property of an owner.[65]

Aristotle justified slavery and differentiation of people according to origin. The slave, in his view, is the property of the slave owner - "live weapon," while slavery is a natural phenomenon where the slave's function is physical work. He thought that manual labor hinders the free development and perfection of the mind, that's why person who is physically exhausted, should not have the right of a citizen. Therefore, he does not distinguish activities of domestic animals and slaves, who serve to satisfy the needs of citizens.[66]

---

[62] Ibid, part 1: 1268a
[63] Aristotle. *Nicomachean Ethics,* 1094b.
[64] Aristotle. *Politics, Part.1:* 1253b.
[65] Ibid: 1253b; 1254a
[66] Ibid: 1252 a; 1253b; 1254 a.

It turns out that Aristotle declared one part of the human being as freely, while the other is slavery. Obviously, "the giant of philosophy" has been misinterpreted in the assessment of slavery. Here's his main ideological credo. But he was ahead to the thinking of his epoch more than centuries: If every weapon could complete the job according to the order or pre-foreseeing, if the textile was torn by himself, and plectri could play independently, then the architects would not need assistants and slaves for concrete.[67]

It turns out that the master would no longer need slaves (i.e., only slavery), if the work tools will do the job according to their own will, or even by the order of the man; Slave manumit is associated with changes in the weapons' production. It is also worth mentioning the fact humane nature of Aristotle- he made a step in his life on the path of slave manumit. In particular, He wrote in the behest and was agree his son Nicomache to the release of several slaves before the death of his father and after their full age, almost all slaves were released.[68]

Aristotle "utopian" prediction that the slogan-economic relations would have shattered by the changes in the production of weapons was justified.

Despite the negative attitude of the ideologists of slave-holding aristocracy toward the monetary economy, Aristotle failed to ignore the phenomena of these events and tried to explain the essence of money, it's value measurements and functions of circulation and accumulation.

Economy and Chrematistic. Aristotle has distinguished between "real wealth" (studying economy) and accumulation of money (chrematistic: trade, breeding, speculation ...), thus confronting each other's economy and chrematism.

In his opinion, the accumulation of property is part of the economy, which is itself or must be gained (economics). No weapon of art is not indefinable either in size or abundance. Art of acquiring property is

[67] Ibid, 1253b.

[68] Aristotle. *Rhetoric*. Tbilisi, 2003, p.11.

natural for economists and politicians, and it is also obviously what is the reason for it.[69]

Aristotle continues to argue on this issue: Economy (leading to family farming) and the art of acquiring property is not the same as one of them deals with accumulation of property and the other for its use. But other than economics, does which field of science study use the necessities of home. Or art of extraction is any part of the economy, or is it something else? In his opinion, for consideration of the science of acquiring property, it is necessary to find out what property is and what its acquisition is ... Concept of property and richness have many parts.[70]

According to him, one part of the accumulated property is essentially part of the economy that exists itself or is acquired (or farming, hunting, fisheries, wars ...) by those who need property to satisfy the required needs, or for social and family relationships (real wealth). However, the property that is needed for a good life does not have an unlimited number of ...[71]

Aristotle speaks here about the "Limitations" of the property (resources-a), and this is a very topical issue even today, because the distribution of limited resources involves many wars and conflicts in modern times.

According to Aristotle, there is another way of accumulating property - the art of money making (chrematistic), which he considered as a means of profit and money. In general, Aristotle is disagreeing with chrematistic, as chrematism explores acquisition of richness in a form of cash.

According to Aristotle's conclusion the "Real Wealth" and the accumulation of money are not the same and differ form each other, the first one is natural and the second is not, because it is the result of some kind of experience and art.[72]

---

[69] Aristotle. *Politics. Part 1:*1256 b.
[70] Ibid, 1256 a.
[71] Ibid, 1256 b.
[72] Ibid, 1257 a.

Discussing the differences between the economics and the chromatistic concepts, and the separation of individual concepts (wealth, property, money accumulation), was an important novelty in the modern era, but in modern reality they are part of both economic (non-profit) activities. Aristotle seemed to be well aware that in terms of division of labor, people are linked to each other through exchange, which is caused by the natural need of humans and in the absence of such demands, there is no exchange. Aristotle, like Xenophon, while analyzing the nature of the goods pointed out that each item can be used for consumption and other purposes. When studying the evolutionary process of the exchange, Aristotle observed the basis - division of labor and noted that the exchange would be when one person needs a product owned by another person - for example, the wine in which it receives bread. It turns out that every property has two types of use: In one case thing is used for a family's needs, in other cases - not; Shoes can be used to wear, for exchanging also, but in both cases the shoes is used.[73]

The basis for exchange was to search for the item's consumer price. If one type of product is incompatible with the other, then their equalization will be occurred in exchanged. The house builder should get his product from the shoe tailor, and the house builder should give him his labor product. This will be implemented with the principle of equality - reimbursement ... In such case it is possible that one "product" cost more than the cost of the second product ... For that purpose, money was created, which measures everything, more and less; Even as many pairs of shoes equals the house.[74] In addition, Aristotle believes that, over time, between different communities arises demand for a variety of specific goods that play the role of money.

Thus, Aristotle related the concept of value with the utility of the subject, and the measurement between the exchanging things with

---

[73] Ibid.

[74] Aristotle. *Ncomachean Ethics,* 1133a.

humans' demand, i.e., if product of the shoe tailor is more demanded in human beings, then shoes should be replaced by more grains.

Aristotle's important merit is that he has analyzed the consumer and exchange values of goods.[75] In a natural (consumer) farming, when all goods are assessed from positions of consumer value, only the genius thinker could truly discover the value of exchanging goods. As noted above, Xenophon and Plato have achieved interesting results in the study of these problems.

Also, the study of the issue of compatibility of commodities in exchange for money, for which Aristotle named the basis - demand, was a genius in that period!

Aristotle does not connect the fine trade with the art of accumulation of wealth, but when other countries joined in exchanging process - gradually developed the art of accumulation of money[76]. He considered three types of trade: marine, transit and retail trade,[77] and they were distinguished from each other by risks.

Generally, Aristotle does not contradict the small trade, in contrast to the big trade, the main field of farming is agriculture, because the exchange product of wheat, fruit-farming, poultry, breeding, beekeeping, and fisheries is possible and justified to accumulate wealth.[78]

It was already noted that the exchanges led to the rise of money amount, which in its turn triggered another way of property accumulation - speculation. However," a giant of thinking" missed when he claimed that "the accumulation of money and the wealth are different ones."[79]

---

[75] Silagadze, A., Atanelishvili, T., Goshadze, G., Demetrashvili, T., Zurabishvili, V. (Then., 2005). *Encyclopedic Dictionary of Economics*. Tbilisi.

[76] Aristotle. *Politics. Part 1:*1257a.

[77] Ibid, 1259 a.

[78] Ibid.

[79] Ibid, 1257b.

Aristotle contradicted another form of property accumulation – usury, which is the reason for the unjust accumulation of money.[80] Aristotle's negative attitudes toward wealth and profit were derived from the society's ideology of that time, as it was considered one of the most important factor of the destruction of the ancient society. He also considered craftsmanship as an accessory activity.[81]

The great thinker geniusly observed the signs of monopoly (especially in trade) and its negative consequences: a man in Sicily purchased the whole amount of metal from metal warehouses with borrowed money, and when merchants came to trade centers, he was only the person who sold iron.[82] Since then, the monopoly problem in the economy has not been eliminated from the agenda.

Overall, Aristotle's views on economic science, property, division of labor, goods, exchange, money, slavery, monopoly and many others represented the peak of the economic thought development of the antiquity slave-holding epoch. They can be summarized as follows:

1. The most profoundly analyzed the socio-economic problems of the ancient epoch and made the basis for the development of economic science and doctrines. He firstly used the term economic science named among the most respected scholars under the policy;
2. Rejected Plato's recommendation on the advantages of common ownership and preferred private property;
3. Family (male and female, parents and children) and settlements are discussed as a cell of social life. The demand for mutual exchange has provided the basis for the relationships of families and communities;

[80] Ibid, 1259 a.
[81] Ibid.
[82] Ibid.

4. He separated special science public relations on politics and explained that politics is a science that organizes a common human life in the state, i.e., it is the art of state governance;
5. He discussed about city-state consisting of ten thousand citizen and distinguished three layers of population: craftsmen, agriculturers and warriors, and also allocated lands in religious, public and private ownership;
6. He considered it fairly a citizen to own property, unfairly –to entrench other's property;
7. Slavery is a natural phenomenon, physical activity is their cast, a disappearance of slavery is linked to possible changes in the production of weapons;
8. Aristotle distinguished two types of riches: "the real wealth" (economics) and "accumulation of money" (chrematistic);
9. He explained the essence of money, the functions of its value measurements, circulation and accumulation. Basis for exchange is division of labor and consumptive value of the item. Without equilibrium of units for change, the exchange can not be made. The money was generated because of difficulty to transport goods in a long distances. Marine, transit and retail trade are distinguished according to their risks. Big trade and usury was condemned.

Aristotle's views on economic, economic categories, slavery and others represents the peak of the economic thinking of the slave-holding epoch, and is the clear proof that the theoretical foundation of economic science takes a deepest origin of the antiquity, that has developed in the later centuries.

2. Epicureanism-Stoicism: Epicurus, Zeno of Citium, Iambulus

Among the philosophical doctrines established on the basis of Hellenistic culture (334-324 BC 30 BC), the most important is Epicureanism and Stoicism.

Epicureanism.[83] The epicureanism was developed by epicure and his like-minded ones. According to this doctrine, maximum happiness is the pleasure of life and liberation from fear of God and death. He denies the importance of social activity. The main thing for him is the individ, on which is depended the public interests. The latter is not a superior goal but a means to achieve personal well-being. The originator of this school is the ancient Greek philosopher Epicurus.

Stoicism.[84] Stoicism's main idea is to be in harmony with nature until the death of man. His followers are aimed to be happy in this world and death fearlessly. Stoicism was also associated with strength and courage. Materialism and individualism are also characterized by Stoicism, which was the most widely recognized philosophy prior to the spread of Christianity in Rome.

Stoicism is a materialistic doctrine that according to which the human soul is a sacred part of his body. The grounds for Stoics teachings coincide with the Epicurus' positions, but there is a difference between them. Stoics have a different understanding of morality. In the sense of the Stoics, all the subjects in the world obey a certain order. This is a divine order - the divinity is a king represented as gods. A person can and should try to keep the order in accordance with his/her personal desires. In this case, the person will be personally more happier. Stoic's doctrine, unlike epicureanism, does not exhort people to restrain their public life.

---

[83] Silagadze, A., Atanelishvili, T., Silagadze, N. (2010). *Economic Doctrines.* Georgian National Academy of Sciences. P.42.

[84] Ibid.

The main representative of Stoicism is Zeno of Citium from Cyprus, Old Romanian Seneca, Marc Aurelius (Emperor) and others. Stoicism is one of the philosophical schools founded by Zeno of Citium (about 300 BC). Sto (Greek στοάποικίλη) - Athens port (a closed gallery created from the columns built at the entrance of the building), where the philosopher Zenongave lessons.

Epicurus. Epicurus (341-270 BC) The ancient Greek philosopher, atheist, was born on the island of Samos. From the age of 14 he began to study philosophy - including Democrit's views, from the age of 18 he listened to Peripatians in Athens. In his writings should be outlined the work written in 37 books on "Nature", only part of which is preserved.

The philosopher Epicurus in Athens did not share Plato's and Aristotle's ideas. According to his belief, each individual can find the keys of wisdom without the aid of the state. This kind of views were very popular when the early political ideals of Greece were gradually forgotten.

Epicurean philosophy is based on four main principles: not to fear the gods (1); Do not care for death (2); Kindness is easily achieved (3) and evil is easily passed though (4).

Epicurus' peculiarity was derived from its materialistic and atheistic worldview. In the sense of it: the world consists of material atoms, based on their connection are derived truly existing, visible bodies, and they are only truly existed; The gods do not participate in the processes in the material world

Epicurus recognized eternity and eternity of the universe; Recognizing the principles of the democratus, to which in turn added the existence of the difference in the form of atoms and made random deviations from the principle of freedom of democratus. According to him, the atomic vertically moving atoms at a vortex can go out from the straight line and collide with each other.

Epicurus, as the head of the hedonism, seeks the basics of good and happy people. He made the existence of the gods, but defined their place in the interstellar space. He demonstrated people from the fear of the gods as free persons. He didn't refer accidentally to epicure followers as "godless." This is one of the reasons why K. Marx named him as an educator of the Epicurus antiquity epoch in his doctoral dissertation ("Difference between Naturphilosophies of Democritus and Epicurus", 1841).[85]

According to Epicurus: Man, like every sensitive person, sees happiness in joy, but if he wants to achieve happiness - should not be satisfied with the first achievement. He should look for ways to make a lasting happiness. For example, he should be especially cautious in love, avoid a rigid political life, to refuse the belief that raises only the fear in man's spirit, Instead of godly devotion, he must enjoy the joy and goodness of his friend, and, in general, be self-restrained.

Thus, according to the doctrine of epicurism: the greatest happiness is the pleasure of life, the exemption from the fear of God and death; Social activity is not so important; Public interest depends on an individ, which is not a superior goal but a means to achieve personal well-being;Each individual could find the wisdom without the aid of the state; Fear of God, indifference to death, goodness is easily achievable and it is easy to pass through the evil; The world is composed of material atoms, which are connected differently and based on this arise visible bodies. The gods do not participate in processes occurring in the material world; The world is eternal and infinite; The principles of democritus are accaptable, but he has made random deviations from him; The place of the gods is in the interstellar space, person who is free from the fear of the gods is free; The happiness of the human being is joy, but if it is to achieve happiness –shouldn't be satisfied with the very first achievement - you should look for a way to have a lasting happiness.

Zeno of Citiumas noted is a founder of Stoicism (336-264 BC). It is known that Zeno's father frequently traveled to Athens, where he

---

[85] Silagadze, A., Atanelishvili, T., Silagadze, N. (2010). *Economic Doctrines*. Georgian National Academy of Sciences. PP.266-267.

brought philosophers works (mostly of Socrates) for his son. Once upon a time of the accident, the child was forced to go to Athens. Here he bought "Essays of Socrates" in the bookstore and asked where Socrates was. After interviewing him a bit about philosophy, Zeno stayed in Athens and began to study philosophy deeply.

The main "Cosmopolitan" ideas of Stoicism are presumably presented in the work "Republic". In it the author presents the world without dividing it into separate states where people are only connected with love.[86]

Zeno discusses very interestingly about economics in his composition "Nature".[87] In the second chapter of the same compostionon "Practice":[88](practice) is an economic, ethical, political subject; Economics is divided into moderate (regulation of interests), regulatory (moderate wealth) and family farming (to achieve well-being).

Zeno, despite the different positions in individual issues, is named among the Epicurus followers. It is not accidentally, that Cicero called him the main epicurean. Only his lectures compiled by Zeno's student are saved. His lecture records are only compiled by Zenon's disciple. Zeno's followers further developed his views.

Iambulus. The ancient Greek writer, Stoicos Iambulus[89] (Old Greek Ἰάμβουλος; 3rd c. BC) figures the land near Ecuador "Island of the Sun", where there is a common non-private property, full equality, labor liberty and people are not divided into layers. These ideas were later reflected in views of Mori T. and Campanella T.

It turns out that in the 3rd c. BC, Greek stoics propagated Plato's "Communist" ideas.

---

[86] https://iphlib.ru/greenstone3/library/collection/newphilenc/document/HASHbb6fc2e9803279862096bb

[87]. Perevod S. Arevshatyan. (1956). *Zenon iz Kitiya. O Prirode* [*Zeno from Kitia. About nature*]. Translation by S. Arevshatyan (1956). http://www.matenadaran. am/ftp/data/Banber3/19.S.Arevshatyan.pdf. *(In Russian).*

[88] Ibid, Chapter 2, p. 329.

[89] Winston, D. (1976). Iambulus' Islands of the Sun and Hellenistic Literary Utopias, *Science Fiction Studies*, №10 = Vol. 3, Part 3/11.

Thus, according to Stoicism's main idea: the human beings should be in harmony with nature before death and thus achieve happiness in this world and the fearless death; Stoics, unlike epicureanism, do not recomend people to restrain in their public life. Zeno is trying to prove a cosmopolitan idea of the possibility of existence of the world without dividing it into classes, in which all people are connected to each other with love; Zeno in a composition on "Nature" represents economics on the one hand as a practical science, on the other hand it is divided into moderate (regulation of interests), regulatory (richer possessions) and family farming (to achieve well-being); Cicero, names Zeno among the epicure followers, despite the different positions in individual issues. Stoics Iambule, in the "Islands of the Sun," favors the existence of common property, humanity without any division into classes, which means Plato's "Communism" propaganda.

3. Ancient Rome

Old Rome's slave holding system, Reaches its blossoming culmination in II-I centuries. At that time, thanks to the powerful wars, ensured the countries economy with a lot of slaves. Huge number of workers has provoked the ground that the slave is only a talking tool. However, in Roman slave holding Latifundia (large private land), when exploitation of the slave had reached its climax of development, the relationship between slaves and owners became tensed, productivity of slave labor decreased.

Antiquity in Ancient Rome is often a peculiar continuation of the Greek antiquity, especially in slavery, but the problems of Rome's slavery are more evident. The issue to change attitude towards slaves ("talking weapon") and reorganization of Roman economy was on the agenda.

Colonat (old Latin colonatus-the form of the dependence of villagers on the land owners) was in the foreground. Initially, the owner of the land had been working on the ground on himself. Subsequently large landowners have begun to lease their lotfundia. The tenants were referred toas coluns, while the lease itself has a monetary form, natural boon was although remain.

The introduction of new mechanisms for managing in old Roman economy would increase productivity. In the end, the structural changes in the management of the economy and change of dependence on the slave have been reflected in the ancient Roman economic thinking.

3.1. Cato on Agriculture

The ideologist of the ancient Roman monarchy, public figure, commander – Cato the Younger (234-149 BC) was from plebeian family (Latin plebius – low class representative in Rome, personally free but without any rights). Carthage's enemy endured his speech in the Senate: "Carthage should be destroyed". (Carthage was located in north Africa, modern Tunisian territory).[90]

Cato is an outstanding political figure and author of the treatise "On Agriculture" (De Agri Cultura)[91] written in the Latin language. He was a landowner and a person with some experience in this field.

Cato's work on "Farming" – represents practical guide to the management of Rome's agriculture at that time. The treatise is one of the oldest amongst the works that are specially devoted to the development of Rome's agriculture. It analyzes the experience of this field. His analysis provides an opportunity to deepen in the economic life of that.

Cato prefers agriculture as compared to other fields of activity. Based on personal experiences, it provides recommendations for

[90] Plutarch, *The Parallel Lives. The Life of Cato the Elder.* http://penelope.uchicago.edu/Thayer/E/Roman /Texts/Plutarch/Lives/Cato_Major*.html#27

[91] Mark Porcius Cato. *Agriculture.* Latin text and translation http://penelope.uchicago.edu/Thayer/E/Roman/ Texts/Cato/De_Agricultura/home.html

efficient management of the estate. Main attention is paid to the production of bread, wine and oil. The income from farming is considered to be the most sacred. For him, people employed in this field are the most reliable.[92]

He criticized trade and usury, but couldn't ignore issues of research in goods-related relation. Merchants are enterprising persons for him. However, in order to earn income, it sometimes justified trading - the sale of unnecessary products (as well as elderly slaves) and the purchase of goods that could not be produced in their homeland. In order to get benefit, he was not categorically against of issuing money as a loan. money laundering. As it is known he was also trading himself and issued loans. [93]

According to Cato's recommendation it is more effective in producing goods near the key markets, including the "rich city, sea or river ...".[94]

It is true that in the above-mentioned discussions, there is still not discovered differential rent, but it is undoubtedly the basis for research in this direction.

Cato was looking for efficient means of exploitation for the improvement of Latifundia's economics. According to him, the slave had no right to behave badly and the owner could not have the right to blame him, slave although had to work in bad weather, but an owner should create basic living conditions for his slave. It was also possible to use the hired slave with cash or natural remuneration.[95]

In the history of economic thinking, Cato's Treatise on "Agriculture" is also noteworthy that it deals with lease relationships and lease liabilities: manage the farm and give the landowner an important part of income and, etc.

---

[92] Ibid, Chapter 1.

[93] Plutarch. *The Parallel Lives. The Life of Cato the Elder*. http://penelope.uchicago.edu/Thayer/E/Roman/ Texts/Plutarch/Lives/Cato_Major*.html

[94] Mark Porcius Cato. *Agriculture*. Chapter 1.

[95] Ibid, Chapter: 4; 5.

Thus, the Cato's Treaty on "Agriculture" is an important source of study of old Roman agriculture, in which, on the one hand, the natural relationship of the ancient era is saved and on the other hand is somehow approved trade-exchange transactions.

Overall: "Agriculture" – is one of the oldest practical manuals of Roman agriculture at that time; Cato's recommendations provide for the management of the estate efficiently - the production of bread, wine and oil, and incomes generated from it to be regarded as the most holy and persons working there – the most reliable ones. Cato criticized the big trade and the usury, but he did ignore over the research of goods-money relations, moreover he participated in this activity; According to Cato's recommendation, it is more effective to produce good near key-markets, the use of hired labor (except slaves) in a labor process (for cash or natural remuneration), definition of lease relationship and lease liabilities.

3.2. Varro "on Agriculture"

Problems of the development of slave-holding agriculture were reflected in the works of old Roman thinkers – Varro (116-27 BC) and Columella. Treatise "On Agriculture" ("Res rusticae" written in 37 years BC)[96] is composed of three books written in the the form of dialogue. Part I of the book is dedicated to farming, part II – stock-breeding, and part III - poultry-beekeeping-fisheries. The author began writing the treatise at the age of 80 and dedicated the book to his wife

The treatise relies on the author's experience and the antiquity literature about the problem under research.

Many of the opinions expressed in the work appear modern. For example, in the opinion of the author, it is favorable if you sell your production to your neighbor and buy from him what you need, it is

[96] *Marcus Terentius Varro on Agriculture*. http://penelope.uchicago.edu/Thayer/E/Roman/Texts/Varro/de_Re_Rustica/1*.html#note36

good for your economy. If it is not enough bread, wine, and others you should bring it from outside, and on the contrary, many of the products should be sold out – outside, it is more useful;Near Rome (and at all in the market), it is more favorable for the development of gardening and horticulture, not in distant places, since transportation from one place to another can damage the product.[97]

It is important that, in Varro's ideas expressed in the ancient era, were more or less identifiable elements of economic doctrines such as: absolute and comparative advantages, foreign trade principles, importance of location and transportation in trade, the basis of differential rent.

Overall, even the above-mentioned opinions expressed twenty one centuries before are absolutely enough to immortalize the author, regardless of its irrelevant interpretation.[98]

The second book of Varro is about the basis of stock-breeding and its great importance; In ancient times it was not shame to be a shepherd and the sheep were very expensive also. One of the interesting examples is Colchi: Aietes, the Argonauts who traveled to the "Golden Fleece".

According to him, Stock-Breeding, as science learns to buy and sell animals, which aims to get maximal revenue; The foundation of all riches is the animal.[99] In addition, he considers that the market price fluctuations are instantly reflected in the development of stock-breeding. The impact of the changes in price on the development of the sector is obviously modern.

Varro in the third book (poultry-beekeeping-fisheries) characterizes the importance of farming for human existence and does not accidentally use the expression "land is mother ...".[100] In his opinion, the following main tasks are facing the science of farming: study of soil

---

[97] Ibid, Book 3.
[98] Ibid, Book 2: 6, 7.
[99] Ibid, Book 2: 1:11; 12.
[100] Ibid, Book 3: 1:5.

composition; Knowledge of land-processing tools; Selection of period for land cultivation and knowledge of what is good to be sown in a land.[101]

It connects separation of the fields of farming and livestock with the shepherds: they lived together and worked there, but when they were enriched, the scale of their production increased and their works were separated.[102]

Varnon is for strengthening the exploitation of slaves and as Old Greek thinkers equals slaves with "talking weapons".[103] For a slave holder, slave is a "thing" and theoretically does not differ from the animal. However, the history made Varro to say that the person is a human being and they should have living conditions and should be able to create a family and have a small amount of property.[104]

Like Plato and Aristotle, it did not favor purchase of slaves from the same tribe (speaking in other language then Latin) and concentrating them together, it would become the cause of disorder in the household.[105]

According to Varen's recommendation, landowners should prefer invited specialists from outside then just slave-specialists and they should create normal conditions of life for them.[106]

On the whole, Varro demanded a strict supervision over them to increase productivity of slaves.

Varro's treaty was written after Spartacus' rebellion and was not accidental to recommend: to actively encourage the hard workers, to care for their reproduction - for this purpose to grant them the right to marry.

Varro has played a significant role in establishing Latifundia economics and in the development of the Roman economic thinking.

---

[101] Ibid, Book 1: 5: 3; 4.
[102] Ibid, Book 3: 1:7; 8.
[103] Ibid, Book 1: 17:1.
[104] Ibid, Book 1: 17: 6; 7.
[105] Ibid, Book 1: 17: 5.
[106] Ibid, Book 1: 16:4.

Overall, Varro's economic thinking is quite interesting:

(a) It was based on his experiences and antiquity literature existing in that period about research problems;
(b) It strengthens the basis for development of the economic concepts such as: Absolute and comparative advantages, foreign trade principles, location and transportation in trade, differential rent;
(c) Consider the priority of livestock as a field, science, and also reaserching its tasks (analysis of the composition of soil, selection of tools and favorable time of cultivation, determining the production of the most favorable products on land).
(d) Focusing on the impacts on realization of animal husbandry products;
(e) He connects the separation of farming and breeding fields to the expansion of shepherds;
(f) He approves strengthening of slave exploitation and equals slaves with "speaking arms" and so forth.

Finally, Varen has played an important role in establishing Latifundia farming and in development of the Roman economic thinking; Evolution of his economic views also caused by rebellion of slaves led by Spartacus.

3.3. Columella "Twelve Volumes"

Lucius Junius Modiretus Columella (4-70years BC.) served in military service in the youth, and then was engaged in agriculture. He was an author of treatise "On agriculture" (Latin"De re rustica", approximately 42 year),[107]consisting of twelve-volume based on antiquity literature. It reflects crisis of slave-holding latifundia farming and ways to overcome it.

In the treatise the book I is dedicated to the general issues of agriculture, book II - soil processing and fertilization, book III - V - viticulture and gardening, book VI - cattle, book VII - VIII - poultry and fisheries, book IX - beekeeping and hunting, Book X-XI - gardening and book XII is about supervisor's rights and duties.

Columella noticed impacts from Latifundia production on Italian agriculture and the inefficiency of slave labor. That's why he demanded to change attitude towards slavery. Namely: An owner should care for every person; Workers in colonats should be treated well. Consequently, where the land is well cultivated, good income is expected.[108]

He was for colonate(for form of attitude of rural population toward large landowners). However, the considers colonate as a supportive form of production that could have been able to modernize a lot of latifundia farm. Such position of Columella was explained by the fact that Latifundia were still strongly rooted in the economic life of Rome, and the colonist gradually stood up and gained strength.

Columella noticed how disagreements between slaves and slave-owners were concerned about, how slave labor and weapons were being treated. In order to overcome these obstacles, a complex of measures that could make the slave possible in a relatively calm environment. For this purpose, he raised the issue: the necessity of division of slave labor, the release women with three and more children from slavery (sometimes slavery) and, etc. He also demanded appointments of distinguished, middle-aged, strong man from their slaves as a supervisor.[109]

---

[107] *Columella: Extant Works*. http://penelope.uchicago.edu/Thayer/E/Roman/Texts/Columella/de_Re_Rustica /Praefatio*.html

[108] Ibid, Book 1: 7:1.

[109] Ibid, Book 1: 8:2.

Columella was for development of lease and livelihood relations. In contrast, he was contrary to lease a land very often, especially to city residents, who did not cultivate the land himself[110], but his slaves did it.. If you can not cultivate the land itself, then it is better peasant to work there[111]. In places where the owner will not be able to cultivate land, it can be leased.[112]

Coluella also requires the land cultivation near the market. He, as a proponent to use colonats widely, advises owners to transfer land to the free colonies. The economic views of Columella reflect the socioeconomic contradictions of the society that tried to be overcome through colonats, but this was no effective way out of the existing natural relations. The thing is that in the conditions of slavery, labor for free citizens was unacceptable, the number of people who suffered after wars has decreased, the problems of workforce increased and the way out was - the formation of new socio-economic relations.

3.4. Pliny the Elder: "Natural History"

The old Roman writer and poet Gaius Plinius is the head of the well-known scholar of old Roman agrarian problems (Latin Gaius Plinius Secundus, approx. 22-79). He is the author of the encyclopedic work "Natural History"[113] (c. 77-78), originally composed of 36 books. While working on it, the author used the works of Varro and his other predecessors. One part of Gaius' works is dedicated to the issues of geography (including the Caucasus), the second - agriculture (planting, breeding, poultry, forestry, fisheries ...), third part - manufacturing of

---

[110] Ibid, Book 1: 7:3.
[111] Ibid, Book 1: 7:4.
[112] Ibid, Book 1: 7:7.
[113] *Pliny the Elder, The Natural History*, John Bostock, M.D., F.R.S., H.T. Riley, Esq., B.A., Ed. http://www.perseus.tufts.edu/hopper/text?doc=Perseus%3Atext%3A1999.02.0137&redirect=true

medicines, precious stones, metals, etc. Many of his opinions are also relevant in modern times.

When discussing agriculture issues, Pliny Head expresses some noteworthy considerations. In his opinion: the noble and honorable man is a one to cultivate land as required. The efficient management of the economy provided a huge amount of grain crops in Italy, which helped to reduce prices on these products.[114]

In his view, (agrees with Kato), the most income sector is viticulture, and then gardening - especially near towns.[115] There are also naturally interesting opinions expressed here: the income earned by fewer expenses is the best. The owner should try to sell as many products as possible to provide additional income;[116] Good land cultivation is beneficial, but unnecessary expenditure on it is worthless;[117] In the process of land cultivation, the more labor will be under strengthened control of the owner, without any other expenses, the more revenues will be.[118]

The market was given the "Equalizer" function of commodities.[119] Name of the money was connected with the goods (Pecus). He names the sheep and then the bull to have a role of money and it is not accidentally[120]. These opinions meant stimulating the deepening of livelihood relations!

Pliny the Elder criticized Latifundia, who restricted the development of Italy and its provinces.[121] It gives great importance to the selection of slave's supervisor who should be a loyal, experienced and authoritative to the owner.[122]

summarizes the economic views of Pliny the Elder:

---

[114] Ibid, Book 18: 11, 15 :19.
[115] Ibid, Book 18: 29.
[116] Ibid, Book 18: 30.
[117] Ibid, Book 18: 38.
[118] Ibid, Book 18: 42.
[119] Ibid, Book 19:56.
[120] Ibid, Book 18:11-12.
[121] Ibid, Book 18: 35.
[122] Ibid, Book 18: 36.

(a) Effective management of land ensures harvesting and reducing price on products;
(b) The most profitable sector is viticulture and then gardening near the following cities;
(c) The best is the income received without additional expenses;
(d) The owner of the product must sell more products, which provides more income;
(e) Good land cultivation is beneficial, but unnecessary expenditure on it is worthless;
(f) In the process of land cultivation, the more labor will be under strengthened control of the owner, without any other expenses, the more revenues will be.
(g) Market can equalize goods;
(h) The name of money is related to the goods. Initially, the sheep played the function of money, then the bull;
(i) Latifundia restricted the development of Italy and its provinces.

3.5. "Concept of Natural Rights": "The Letters" of Cicero and Seneca

The "Concepts of Natural Rights" was developed by Cicero in the first century BC. I developed a century. According to this conception, the public norms, for their natural grounds, are all equal to all members. According to this concept, public norms due to their natural grounds, refers equally to all members of society. Such an approach was, in fact, an attempt to interact with Plato's and Aristotle's philosophies.

It seems that Cicero also support the equality of human beings, but it also speaks about people with low levels of "moral nature" and involved in physical labor. It is against labor to get profit, but in this case large traders and bankers are not the meant.

Cicero defended private property and large land ownership of latifundists and lenders. Priority for him was development of farming.

His attitude towards usury is of dual character: On the one hand, giving money as a loan is a harmful event for a man, and on the other hand, it does not favor the movement against usury. Such position of Cicero was conditioned by contradictions between the natural and commodity relations of the old Roman economy.

Marcus Tulius Cicero (Latin: Marcus Tullius Cicerō, 106-43 BC), an ideologist of aristocracy in Rome, was a colorful figure of world history, brilliant orator, writer, advocate, famous philosopher, state actress, ideologist of the slave era.

Cicero's Dialogues: "On the Commonwealth" and "On the Laws"[123] (Latin: De re publica; De Legibvs), Is an important source of antioxidant polit-economic thinking.

Dialogues "On the Commonwealth" (approximately in c. 54 BC) consists of six books. Among them are the forms of best arrangement of the State (Book 1-2), the essence of the state, the role of justice (Book 3-4) and the best state figures (Book 5-6).[124]

Cicero considered Plato and Aristotle as the greatest philosophers, but did not like "Plato's common property". Like Aristotle and Stoics, he believes that civil society is derived from natural conditions and all people are equal, property differences are not the result of private ownership, but also the relationships developed in society. He linked the origin of the private property with the hereditary, the wars, the laws and, etc. Austerity was nominated as a source of income growth.[125]

Cicero discussed three forms of state structure: democracy, aristocracy and monarchy. In his opinion, all forms of governance have shortcomings and it is best to use the fourth form of governance

---

[123] M. Tvlli Ciceronis. Dialogi. De re publica; De Legibvs [Dialogues of republic; From Legibus]... Oxford University Press, 1966. file:///C:/Users/user/Downloads/Preview_Cicero,_J._G._F._Powell_ed._M._Tulli_Ciceronis_De_Re_Publica,_De_Legibus,_Cato_Maior_de_Senectute,_Laelius_de_Amicitia.pdf; (*Цицерон. Диалоги о государстве, о законах. Москва, 1966*) [(*Cicero. Dialogues about the state, about the laws*. Moscow 1966)].

[124] Ibid.

[125] *De re publica* [*To publish*]. Book IV: VII (7).

established on the basis of all three forms of state structure (Book 1).[126] Cicero's political sympathy is an aristocratic republic, the basis of which is justice and not only the unity of free people (like Plato and Aristotle). He connects the concept of law connects with the universal laws of nature. The state is a human equisition that is related to the interests of law and the public.[127]

Cicero believes that "Natural Justice" (Book 4) is expressed well in Roman state, but in some cases (Book 2) injustice is useful for the state, in some cases (Book 3) it is not; On the earth civil society was formed based on human consensus.[128] It must be governed by either one of the king's government or some of the best personalities elected by the Senate or the public authorities.[129]

Cicero developed the concept of "Natural Rights"[130] in his work " on laws" in which the "Natural Law" is common to all human beings. Nature has created man for justice so that people can benefit from fair principles;[131] Living in harmony with nature - is superior welfare. He is living in harmony with kindness. In general, the mother of well-being – wisdom.[132]

So, Cicero:

(a) Protected private property and large land ownership of latifundists and gombeen-men;
(b) Usury - lending money to borrow money is considered a harmful event for the purpose of receiving benefits but does not support the movement against him;

---

[126] Ibid, XXIX, 45.
[127] Ibid, XXV, 39.
[128] Ibid, Book I, XXV, 39
[129] Ibid, XXVI, 41.
[130] Ibid, De Legibvs. Book 1. X, 28.
[131] Ibid.
[132] Ibid, XXII, 58.

(c) Shares the idea of natural origin of the state, do not like the overall property of everything;
(d) Recognizes the "natural equality" of human beings and the difference in property;
(e) The origin of private property is connected with heritage, wars, laws and so on;
(f) The best way to get income is austerity;
(g) Approve the legal-based Aristocratic Republic, the concept of "Natural Right";

Lucius Annaeus Seneca. Crisis in the way of slavery production was severely reflected in the views of Romanus writer, philosopher and public figure Lucius Anuaeus Seneca (Latin: Lucius Annaeus Sĕnĕca minor, 4 - 65 years cordova, Spain). He was, as Nero's educator and one of the chief figures of stoicism, had a significant impact on the ideology of the Roman community. He was the son of Lucius (Mark) Annaeus Seneca, an outstanding historian. It is known that Seneca, death sentenced bu the order of Nero, finished her life with a suicide. Despite her categorical resistance, his wife Pauline also committed suicide with her husband.

According to Seneca: "By nature" all people are equal, including slaves, but they should not be treated like animals. He understood the danger of slavery and demanded a more mild attitude towards them. In addition, he reminded the slave owners how many people were killed by their slaves. However, unlike Aristotle, he did not see the need to release slaves.

Thus, Seneca is in the position of maintaining essentially slavery, but he feels the upcoming threat and tries to stop it with using more flexible methods.

Seneca condemned usury (as it is said, he took part in this activity and accumulated a lot of money); He criticized the defects of the slogan, but his alternative was not offered. Seneca's views influenced

Christianity, as it defended the idea of spiritual equality of all human beings.

Seneca's economic views are more detailed in the work "Moral Letters of Lucilius" (hereinafter - Letters).[133] Seneca advocates the idea of equality between women and men. Besides, strongly condemns the gladiators' fight as a show of spectators that ends with the killing of the warrior.[134]

According to Seneca, wealth is the cause of evil, not because of it is evil on its side, but because it pushes people to do evil. Consequently, wealth can be the reason for welfare and evil.[135]

Seneca analyzes the following provisions of the Stoics: Wisdom is Worthy, to be a wise man- No; Goodwill benefits only under the enactment; Wise man is the owner of wisdom and he is only a good man.[136]

As it was mentioned, he condemned usury: Gombeen-man won't give an amount even to his relatives without a 12% interest rate.[137] Nevertheless, it is necessary to start a business and get a better loan directly and not with a mediator. Wisdom is always looking for natural wealth; Revenue can also be obtained through good knowledge of trade - by correctly selecting the requested goods and marine routes.[138]

Seneca reviews the money negatively and recognizes her only accumulation function. In his opinion, money does not make anyone rich, on the contrary, only stirs up a great desire of acquisition - for who has more money, has more opportunity.[139]

Senica, as a stoicist, has had some influence on Christian religion. Finally, his views can be summarized as follows:

---

[133] *Moral Letters to Lucilius*: Vol.1-1917; Vol. 2 – 1920; Vol. 3 – *1925*.
[134] Ibid, Vol.1. Letter 7:3-5.
[135] Ibid, Vol. 2. Letter 87: 31, 32, 33.
[136] Ibid, Vol. 3. Letter 117: 1, 2, 8, 9.
[137] Ibid, Vol. 3. Letter 118: 2.
[138] Ibid, Vol. 3. Letter 119: 1, 5, 6.
[139] Ibid, Vol. 3. Letter 119: 9, 10.

(a) By nature all men are equal, including slaves. They are human beings and they should not be treated like animals. Like Aristotle he did not discuss slavery;
(b) Condemned usury and the high rate of interest, it is better to take a loan directly and not with the mediator;
(c) Criticized the defects of the slave-holding regime, without the suggestion of its alternative;
(d) Defending the idea of equality of women and men;
(e) Strongly condemned the gladiators' battle;
(f) Wealth, is a cause of welfare as well as evil;
(g) Goodwill benefits only under the enactment;
(h) Trade is a good way of getting revenue;
(i) Recognized for money only accumulation function.

Finally, it was forgotten the view about privilege of polis prevailing in Greece, and the notion of "natural law" in Roman culture as well.

3.6. The Agrarian Reform Projects of Brothers Gracchus

By the 2nd century BC, there were many problems of vital interest in Rome. This era has been closely linked to large land ownership - increase of latifundia, increase of impoverished workers, and strengthening the fight against land and slavery. In addition, the natural farming increasingly became of commodity character, that could be a source of profit. Agriculture products often were a subject of buying-selling that stimulated the scope of this sphere.

In Rome, the Agrarian-Democratic Movement was led by the representatives low-level class – Gracchus Brothers. The brothers had achieved significant success in youth.

Tiberius Gracchus. Tiberius Gracchus (Latin Tiberius Sempronius Gracchus, c. 163-133), an old Roman political figure, the older brother of Gaius, popular tribune (134 years till the death). Immediately after the election of the People's Tribune, the agrarian reform project was introduced. It envisaged limiting the use of public lands for large land owners. This was a novelty since the lands were to be distributed.

Tiberius dreamed of Rome free from slavery. B. Year In 133, he was elected to the People's Tribunal (a high-ranking official elected from the People). He proposed to the people's assembly an agrarian reform project which banned land ownership to have over 1000 jugerum (approximately 250 ha, without paying the rent) for the family.[140] The rest of the land was to be transferred to the state, from which no more than 5-30 juger (approximately 1.5-7.5 ha) should have been distributed to the poor. It was allowed to transfer these lands as an inheritance, but their sale was forbidden.[141]

Tiberius' project also implied a certain amount of money for farmers to purchase seed material, inventory, etc. To buy. Such a bill was relatively fair in that era, but it was still difficult to approve in the Senate. The richest people (who for centuries have been using public lands without any fees) were strongly resistant to this issue.

According to Greek historian Plutarch (Greek Πλούταρχος, Latin Mestrius Plutarchus, about 46-127), Tiberius at the people's council while describing of the difficult economic situation of Italian workers it was noted that in Italy, even the animals have shelters, while those who fight for Rome and sacrifice their lives have nothing more than air and light in their country, they are homeless. Commanders deceive soldiers when calling them to the fight in order to protect the graves of their ancestors that the majority of Romans did not have! Soldiers are

---

[140] [140] Lapyryonok, R. *Nasledie Agragrnogo Zakona Tiberiy Grakxa: Zemelni Vopros I Politicheskaya Borba V Rime 20-X Gg. II V. Do N. E. [The Legacy of the Agrarian Law of Tiberius Gracchus: A Land Question and Political Struggle In Rome, the 20th Gg. II B. To N. E]* http://www.rumvi.com/products/ebook/наследие-аграрного-закона-тиберия-гракха-земельный-вопрос-и-политическая-борьба-в-риме-20-х-гг-ii-в-/f4443ebb-896b-423a-9a37-22cdf561422e/preview/preview. Html. *(In Russian)*

[141] Roselaar, S. (2010). *Public Land in the Roman Republic: A Social and Economic History of Ager Publicus in Italy*, 396–89 BC. — Oxford: Oxford University Press.

fighting and die for the luxury and riches of others, and in fact "The Rulers of the World", don't have even a small piece of land! [142]

The People's Assembly adopted the Agrarian Bill of Tiberius Gracchus and he led the Land Distribution Commission. In the course of reform process, the situation was tense. As a result, Tiberius and his many supporters were killed in 133 year BC.

Tiberius Gracchus' sacrifice has not gone without result. For example, about 2 million juger land was distributed in accordance with its draft law.

Gaius Gracchus. Tiberius Gracchus's death situation was still tensed. Tiberius's way was continued by his brother, the old Roman politician Gaius Gracchus (Latin Gaius Sempronius Gracchus, 153-121). He was elected at People's Tribunal in 123 year BC.

Gaius's goal was to bring his brother's initiatives to the end. During his period of work, there have been many useful things in Rome: new streets and bread wares were built; Each Roman citizen was given bread at half an amount per month. He demanded a reduction in military service and the soldiers to be dressed at the expense of the treasury.

More specifically, during the period of Gauss:

- Bread law, which provided bread to be sold for the poor of Rome a bit cheaply;
- Road law, according to which the new roads in Italy should be built, making it easier for the small landowners who emerged as a result of Tiberius reforms;
- The court law, in which judges included low level representatives of low level class;
- The military law that made military service easier for the poors, and in particular the military equipment was no longer paid by them;

[142] Plutarch, *The Parallel Lives. The Life of Caius Gracchus*. http:// penelope. uchicago.edu/ Thayer/E/Roman/Texts/Plutarch/Lives/Caius_Gracchus*.html

The issue of establishment of new land colonies in southern Italy and many there were also determined.

One of the laws of Gaius's Gracchus, one provided distribution of public land; Second (military law) - the recruitment of the soldiers with the clothes and the recruitment of young people aged only 17; Third - granting the right to participate in elections for all residents of Italy; Fourth (about bread) - low prices on bread, fifth (law on judicial proceedings) - cutting senators' rights, etc.

Gaius Gracchus also met with great obstacles on the way to implement measures. The rich (despite some sympathy by Gauss toward them) had begun a fight for dear life. He did not let them alive, so he asked his slave to kill him.

Thus, his brother Gaius Gracchus continued Tiberius' way, during which his were adopted laws about bread, roads, court, military service and others. About the improvement of the conditions of the poor.

That's why lives of hard-working brothers were finished like this. People built the monuments on the site of their work, where they donated and named them as a saint.

Years have passed and many times have changed the rule of Rome in which the rich have tried to diminish the laws of the Gracchus, but Romans did not forget the brothers Gracchi. One or two people in that epoch could not change the essential lifestyle, but the action of the brothers Gracchus strengthened the struggle for justice in the people.

3.7. Slave Rebellion and Economic Ideas of Ancient Christianity

In the 1st century BC, the Latifundia economy of Rome reached the highest level of development. Then their management problems were aggravated and the crisis started. This was natural, because the higher level of slave holding prosperity would have also been threatened result in socio-economic contradictions.

After further strengthening of slave exploitation in Italy, produced the greatest rebellion in the history of antique countries led by Spartak in 74-71 years Spartak (Latin Slapatus, c. 110-71). The main demand for Spartak rebellion was to make slaves free and distributing lands to them. Gold, trade and speculation was unacceptable for the rebels. In this long and lasting chain of battles against the slaveholding regime, this rebellion is the most important, which has are volutionized effect on historical fate of this epoch.

Spartak - Kapiel Slave-Gladiator - After run with a few other slaves, many of the fellow slaves gathered around them. Spartak preferred to die in the fight for freedom then in an arena in front of spectators.[143] According to Plutarch, Spartacus was distinguished with physical strength, as well as with his intellect and humanism.[144]

The rebels captured weapons and achieved many victories. They did not have the exact plan of action. They firstly moved from the south of Italy to the north, then back, but they did not enter in Rome! Finally, they decided to enter Sicily, but in vain, because they could not agree with the ship owners.

Finally, the Roman army defeated them. Spartacus was killed in the fight, and thousands of his supporters were burned at the stake on the way to Capau-Rome. It is true that the rebellion led by Spartak was defeated, but he did not go in vain, moreover, this rebellion so strongly hit to slave holding regime in Rome's, that the latter could not stand on his feet. The deep crisis of Latifundia economy has begun, which led to the rise of colonies and feudal relations.

The most important role in strengthening the economic thinking of this period is Christianity. Early Christianity (I-II cc) demonstrated the interests of the peoples against slavery. His merit was raised the issue on the equality of human beings.

---

[143] Lomouri, N. (1963). *Spartak, Life of outstanding people*. Tbilisi. P. 36.

[144] Plutarch. *The Parallel Lives. The Life of Crassus*, 8. http://penelope.uchicago.edu/Thayer/E/Roman/ Texts/Plutarch/Lives/Crassus*.html

At the same time, early Christianity preached the fairness of one another, the universal necessity of labor; It censured accumulation of great wealth and demanded its redistribution; He condemned usury and also benefit received from it; Denies private property and draws attention to common ownership.

The Bible. The interesting examples of economic thinking are included the Bible (books) comprised of the Old Testament (Judaism, whose lawfulness was in 5-6 CE) and from the new Testament (Christianity recognizes the two parts).

According to the Bible: Payment is obligatory, but it is prohibited to extort; Tax privileges are provided for the priests; The debt was subject to immediate payments in the prescribed time; He recognized the Institute of fidejussor, but at the time required a caution. It also recognized allowed trade and demand its protection; it is also permitted to lend money "Whom you are asking by, give him; And whoever wants to borrow from you, do not turn your back" (them 5.42).

At the beginning of the fourth century, Christianity became the dominant religion in the Roman Empire. The Roman Emperor (from 306 year), Constantine I the Great (285-337) became an obvious advocate of Christianity. Sunday, as the Easter Day of Christ, was named as day-off, the construction of Christian temples began in Palestine, in 324-30 years. Founded Constantinople (instead of Byzantine) and, etc.

By initiative and participation of Emperor Constantine the Great (in 325) The first Ecumenical Council of the World was held in Nicaea (Greek Nikaia, present Isník, Turkey). The Assembly adopted the Law of the Unified Christian Faith, ie. Christianity has been adopted by the prevailing layers and has been declared a state religion. According to the current information, the meeting was also attended by the representatives of the christian organizations densely populated by Georgian - Bichvinta Bishop Stratophile and Bishop Domnus of Trapezun.

The work of the World Ecumenical Councillasted for about two months. Twenty laws were adopted from which under the law number 17 it was prohibited for clergy to receive benefit from lended money.[145] The economic thinking of the slave holding epoch ends in the Old Rome. The downfall of the Roman Empire largely cursed the crisis of the slavery exploitation system, which influenced the further development of economic thinking.

Thus: The crisis of Roman Latifundia economy began in the I century BC, causing colonies and feudal relations; In the struggle against slavery, the rebellion of Spartacus has had a decisive impact on the historic fate of this society; Christianity is a great contributor to strengthening the economic thinking of this period. Early Christianity (I-II cc) demonstrated the rights of persons against slavery, its merit is to promote the idea of equality of people; Early Christianity demanded fair treatment of each other, the universal necessity of labor, the distribution of great wealth, the condemnation of the usury, common ownership on property; According to the Bible: Payment is compulsory, taxable privileges and trade are permissible, usury is forbidden and, etc.

In general, even the modest recommendations of old Rome's empirical economic thinking could not be introduced in practice - economic thinking of slaveholding regime ended in Ancient Rome. Slave rebellions broke the slaveholding regime and incursions of conqueror tribes finished the Roman Empire - in 476, the German Emperor Odoacer (431-493) decrowned the last Emperor of Western Rome Romulus Augustulus (475-476), and the centuries-old domination of the Roman Empire ended.[146]

---

[145] *The laws of the first council of Nicaes.* http://library.church.ge/index.php? option= com_content &view=article&id=147%3A-i-&catid=34%3A2009-12-29-11-31-18&Itemid= 59&lang=ka

[146] Mary T. Boatwright, Daniel J. Gargola, Noel Lenski, Richard J. A. Talbert. (2011). *The Romans: From Village to Empire: A History of Rome from Earliest Times to the End of the Western Empire*. Second Edition.

Chapter 3

NEW VISIONS

During the reign of *Gaius Julius Caesar* (100-44 BC), for German tribes settled on the coast of Rhein the private property on the land was something new. In the occupation tribes of the Roman Empire, rural communities played a major role and the lands were distributed among the members of the community for a certain period of time. It is not accidental that most of the tribes that had been invaded in different countries created rural communities, where the land were jointly used by community members. In parallel, the chiefs gradually assumed the lands and formed the aristocrat of the community owners.

Eventually, the conquering tribes settled on outward side of the Roman Empire, based on which free peasants' class was formed. The rulers of the states established on the ruins of the Roman Empire brought grant conquered land the inhabitants (the "Feeds") close to them and to the distinguished warriors.[1] Peasants along with land cultivation, performed different obligations for new mentors. So the feudal property on land and incomplete ownership on workers - peasants appeared. Thus, the peasant loses freedom and becomes a base estate, who is forced to work in the mentor's land. However, peasants,

---

[1] Reynolds, Susan (1996). *Fiefs and Vassals: The Medieval Evidence Reinterpreted.*

in contrast to the slave, have the tools of production and can manage their private farms with personal labor.

During the Millennial Era - from 476 years (from the fall of the Roman Empire) - until 1453 (before the collapse of Constantinople) - new economic thinking dominated secular and theological fields.[2] Social structure of medieval centuries reflected the problems of regulation of property - mainly land distribution. As noted above, the agrarian reform was still in the forefront in the Roman Empire. In the 5-9 centuries, the free farmers of the community were under the patronage of the lord: small land owners (part of them forced), voluntary united with large landholders to alleviate the tax problems. Large landholders created new jobs for the poors. Gradually the "self-sufficient economy" was established, which was subsequently changed with a more profitable exchange economy - intensive trading. The powerful influence of the church with a great land ownership on the economy should have been taken into consideration, which preached the ideas of production, hardship, loyalty, and obedience.

In the Italian cities - Venice and Genoa, also in several European countries trade has been renewed. Employees created associations to defend their rights here. Industrial enterprises appeared, traded with money (Jews only traded in precious metals in the 9-10 centruries), lombards were subsequently replaced by bankers. The church forbade usury, but its representatives were involved in this activity. These events contributed to the revival of agriculture. The real price of the product became the opportunity to establish justice between the seller and the buyer. Feudal relationships were deepened.

Duration of feudalism was different in different countries. For example, in Western Europe (France, Italy, ...) it developed from the 5th century and continued in the 17th (in England) – 18th (in France) centuries, in Russia - from the 9th to the second half of the 19th century,

---

[2] Silagadze, A., Atanelishvili, T., Silagadze, N. (2010). *Economic Doctrines*. Georgian National Academy of Sciences. P.50.

in Georgia (Kartli, Meskheti ...), from the 6th to the second half of the 19th century.[3]

Feudalism has mainly devoted three stages of development: the earliest early medieval periods of origin and formation of feudalism (5-11 centuries); Second, the late medieval period of the feudalism (11-15 cc) and the third, the period of feudalism and the rise of capitalism (16-17 cc).[4]

In the epoch of early feudalism, the political and economic thinking slid into declined, had seemed to have forgotten the creativity of the ancient thinkers - many important works of the ancient epoch have been lost. (In the Middle Ages only one dialogue by Plato was known as "Timaeus", and discovery of Aristotle's "Politics" by the Arabians had a great impact on the development of political and economic thinking of the 13th century). In fact, the spiritual life was run by the clericals (Latin klerikalis), whose research subject was mainly religious works. The goal of clericalism was to strengthen the Church's influence in the country's political and economic life. Feudal economic relations have been reflected in the works of various countries or in the "codes".

1. Aurelius Augustine: "Fair Price"

One of the most prominent representatives of the early medieval economic thought is the Bishop *Aurelius Saint Augustine* (Latin Aurelius Augustinus; 354-430), a theologian and ecclesiastical figure of the North African (East Algeria, Hippo regius).[5]

The father of Aurelius - Patricius was originally pagan and then was baptized, and Mother-Monika was brought up in Christianity. 17-year-old Augustine left for Carthage to get education. Returning to his

[3] Anchabadze, G. (2005). *History of Georgia. Short sketch.* Tbilisi: Caucasian House.
[4] Silagadze, A., Atanelishvili, T., Silagadze, N. (2010). *Economic Doctrines.* Georgian National Academy of Sciences. p.54.
[5] *Complete Works of Saint Augustine,* http://www.augustinus.it/links/inglese/opere.htm

homeland, Augustine began his pedagogic work. Since then, his world outlook has also changed - 387 baptized in Rome. Aurelio distributed all his belongings to the poor and started working in church: He founded the first women's monastery in Africa.

In terms of economic thinking from the writings of the Blessed Augustus, the following ones attract attention: "about the city of God", "About the Trinity", "On order" and so forth.[6]

Blessed Augustine in his work "On the City of God" (413-427) criticized the vicious parties of public life and urged everyone to be involved in the work, according tothe famous principle of Paul the Apostle: "Who does not work, does not eat". In this work, usefulness of the item is logically named as the evaluation measure of the item. According to the benefit of each person finds in a particular item, there are different standards of value.[7]

In his opinion, the demand is affecting the formation of the price, but it does not apply to slaves: mostly the horse is more expensive than the slave, the precious stone is more expensive than the servant woman[8]. Obviously, such an approach is caused by ideological pressure.

At the same time, it is correct to note that the rarity of the thing constantly increases its price: rarity of art production increases the value of these products.[9]

In the work of Blessed Augustine - "On The Trinity" describes the cost-to-sale process and the desire of most people: "buy cheaply and sell expensively."[10]

When discussing these issues, he used one of the first to use the term "Fair Price". To this end he described a few episodes: First, when the ancient manuscript was offered to his acquaintance, he noticed that the seller did not know the true value of this manuscript and paid him a

---

[6] Ibid.
[7] Ibid, *The City of God*. Book 11-16.
[8] Ibid, *The City of God*. Book 7-3.
[9] Ibid, *On the Trinity*. Book 13. Chapter 3:6.
[10] Ibid.

fair price, which the seller did not expect. Secondly, it is not acceptable, but rarely there is such an embezzler, who sells the inherited property at a lower price than its value and purchases some other property more expensively to meet his demand; Third, he knows people who buy bread expensively for purpose of charity and sell it to their citizens at lower prices, which is good enough.

Aurelius *Sante* Augustine's "Fair Price" concept is somewhat original-progressive, which provides for the rareness, value, philanthropy, charity and demand for a variety of things. This explanation of the problem of pricing was an important novelty in that epoch and such approaches provided the basis for the centuries-old history of the market price formation, the main element of which is demand-supply.

Besides, Blessed Augustine believes: Large trade and usury are unacceptable;[11] The state, in the face of injustice, is the system of domination by one group of people into another;[12] Property differentiation is permissible and the struggle for equalization of property is insufficient; All men are equal to God, which they must meet peacefully; Slavery is a righteous punishment for the sins committed by a man; Slaves are also defeated people in the war who must obey God's judgment. Consequently, slavery is a divine sentence that enables a natural order.[13]

On the whole, economic views of Blessed Augustine can be summarized as follows: He was one of the first who used the term "fair price"; The item's usefulness was logically named as one of the criteria of it evaluation; Demand sets the price; Rarity of the thing constantly increases its price; Expensive person is unacceptable, and the philanthropist is acceptable; Large trade and usury unacceptable;

---

[11]Saint Augustine. *O Poryadke. ["On Order"].* Part 2-5. http://filosof.historic.ru/books/item/f00/s00/z0000107/st001.shtml

[12] Complete Works of Saint Augustine. *The City of God.* Book 4:4.

[13] Ibid, *The City of God.* Book 19:15, 16.

Property differentiation is permissible and the struggle for equalization of property is insane and so forth.

2. "Salic Law": New Legal-Economic Relationships

"Salic Law" (Latin Lex Salica) gives an important information about Frank's economic life in Western Europe. This name is derived from Salian Francs (at that time the franchise included German tribes as well). In particular, francs were divided into two large branches: Sallian, it means francs living at the Rhine embouchement of the fringe francis and répuers, francs living at the upper part of the Rhine.[14]

At this time, private property on land was established in German tribes, the state formed and the different layers of society also; It was necessary to create legal guarantees for property protection. So, the aim this Code was same, which was drawn up in Latin language,[15] supposedly in the 5-6 centuries by Clovis I the King of France (Clov, 466-511).

"Code" constituted legal and economic norms, including penalties:

- For the absence of the court - 15 Solids;[16]
- From stealing goods to 3 - 35 Solids[17] ;
- For stealing the bird - 3 Solids;[18]
- For stealing the property of the slave owner – to return the stolen property and 15 Solids, and for 30 Solids for stealing the slave;[19]

---

[14] *Liber Historiae Francorum* [*French historical*]. http://www.vostlit.info/Texts/rus/Gesta_Fr/frametext.htm

[15] *The Salic Law*. http://avalon.law.yale.edu/medieval/salic.asp

[16] Ibid, Chapter 1-1. Currency rate of that perod Rome: 3 Solid= approximately 1 cow.

[17] *The Salic Law*. Chapter: 2:1; 3:1, 2, 3.

[18] Ibid, Chapter 7:1.

[19] Ibid, Chapter 10:1, 2.

- For debt non-payment - 15 Solid (except the principal amount);[20]
- Confiscation of property without court decision - 200 Solids;[21]
- To remind three times about the obligation to pay the debt: one warning-3 Solids, additional reminder of non-payment - 15 Solids;[22]
- For killing the nobleman - 600 Solid counts, etc.[23]

In addition, according to the Code, it is clear that there was a private farmland and also lands owned by the collective. Sale of arable land was prohibited; The land that was owned by a peasant without an heir (without a son) after the death of his family should be transferred to the community; In the sixth century, was the process of splitting the francs into layers; Community relations had been changed by feudal relationships.

Thus, in the Western Europe, the Salic Code set out new forms of legal and economic relations - responsibilities for theft of property, for non-payment, for killing of human beings, for absence in court; Ownership forms on land, the rule of landless remnants and others.

3. "Instructions About Homelands"

"Instructions about Homelands" ("Capitulare de villis")[24] are drawn in Latin language approximately in 800 year. Based on the Order of the Emperor Franks (from 800 year, from 768-a queen) by the Order of *Carlos the Great* (742-814) It reflects the issues of the management of the early medieval great feudal land ownership, the nature of the

[20] Ibid, Chapter 50:1.
[21] Ibid, Chapter 51:1
[22] Ibid, Chapter 52:1.
[23] Ibid, Chapter 53:1.
[24] *The Capitulare de Villis* [*A chapter in cities*]. https://www.le.ac.uk/hi/polyptyques/capitulare/trans.html

economy of that time (including the craftsmanship). It contains the market and market revenues in feudal frames

Instructions It becomes clear from the "Instructions" that the process of establishing feudal relations in rural areas was never completed.

It is said in some specific "instructions":

- "Homeland" should first satisfy personal need;[25]
- Managers of the "Homelands" should ensure timely cultivation of lands (including vineyards), to harvest without any loss, the creation of high quality seed material;[26]
- Persons, who damaged homelands would have been penalized;[27]
- 1/10 of the harvest was given to the churches of this land;[28]
- How many animals and birds should be grown, as well as the number of cereals, grapes, honey, fish ... must be manufactured in the homeland;[29]
- Local harvest should be enough to satisfy local needs during the whole year;[30]
- Special care should be taken for forest and special parks;[31]
- Allowed to sell the surplus product;[32]
- There should be craftsmen (blacksmiths, also working on gold-silver, shoe tailors, gun specialists, etc.), to prepare necessary things locally at the place[33].

---

[25] Ibid, Chapter 1.
[26] Ibid, Chapter 5:37.
[27] Ibid, Chapter 4.
[28] Ibid, Chapter 6.
[29] Ibid, Chapter 5, 19, 23.
[30] Ibid, Chapter 20.
[31] Ibid, Chapter 36, 46.
[32] Ibid, Chapter 39.
[33] Ibid, Chapter 45.

Thus, “Instructiona about homelands” is another “instruction” in Western Europe about perfection issues of feudal-natural farming of that time, in which the trade and crafts development is encouraged.

4. “Russkaya Pravda”

The Kievan Russ’ was created on the eve of the 8th and 9th centuries, as a result of the merging of east slavic tribes. In this period communal relationships of east Slavs was directly replaced by feudal relationships. The main “class” of population “feudalsi” and peasants were established. Land was the property of Feudal, the economy was characterized by a low level of technique and a natural character.

It is of great importance to study Russian economic thinking of the era through the “Law Collection” entitled as “*Russkaya Pravda”*.[34] There are short and extensive - comparatively late - variants. The “Laws” were created during the *Yaroslav the Wise* (978-1054) and his successor, *Vladimir Monomakh* (1053-1123). It includes old Russian legal and socio-economic issues.

In particular, according to “Russkaia Pravda”:

- If someone had taken the horse without taking permission of his patrons and took his clothes, the weapon was fined at 3 grivna;[35]
- The amount of fines for stealing hay and wood were 9 grivna (separately);[36]
- Individuals for a particularly grave crime was death punished (for murder), but deliberate and accidental offenses were taken into account;

[34] *Russkaya Pravda* [*Russian Truth*]. http://www.hrono.info/dokum/1000dok/pravda72.php

[35] Currency unit 1⁄25 Grivna (10-11cc), 1/50 Grivna (till the beginning 15c); 1 kuna= 2 gr. Silver https://ru.wikipedia.org/wiki/Древнерусская_куна.

[36] *Russkaya Pravda* [*Russian Truth*], Ibid, 11-12.

- The killing of the nobleman was punished with 80 grivna,[37] low-level representatives ("Smerd", "Ridovich" and "Kholopy") –with 5 grivna[38], or 16 times less;
- A fine ("VIRA") should be paid in the monetary units of that period: Grivna and Kuna (1/25 Grivna);
- The following deadlines for loand have been established: short-term and medium-term;[39]
- Established 20% loan interest rates. In case of delay in the loan payment, the loan interest was 50% -100%[40] and, etc.

Apparently, "Russkaya Pravda", besides the nobility, defended the interests of merchants and artisans from the arbitrariness of the mediators. It is known that the Kiev rebellion (1113) caused by social contradictions was put down by Vladimir Monomagh, but it was necessary to implement some economic measures. For example, it is not accidental that according to "Russkaya Pravda", 20% of the maximum benefit of expenditure was determined.

Thus, "Russkaya Pravda" is the first law collection set up in "Kievan Rus", in which criminal norms and norms of civil law are stated, namely regulation of monetary credit.

5. Shota Rustaveli: "The Knight in the Panther's Skin"

The immortal poem "The Knight in the Panther's Skin" was written by *Shota Rustaveli* (1160/65 - 1210/1213) of the great Georgian poet, 1189-1207/1210/1213 in Georgia during the reign of Queen Tamar in

[37] Ibid, P.39.
[38] *Russkaya Pravda* [*Russian Truth*]. Ibid: 21-22-23.,
[39] Ibid, 47.
[40] Ibid, 47, 48, 49.

Georgia (1189-1207/1210/1213), it attracts the attention of specialists with its high level economic thinking.

The vizier of the Queen Tamar (c. 1160-1213) was also responsible for caring for the Jvari Monastery (Georgian monument) in Jerusalem, where the great poet had spent the last years of his life and was buried there. It is not accidental that portrait of the great Shota Rustaveli depicted in the Jvari Monastery of Jerusalem.

"The Knight in the Panther's Skin" occurs such economic opinions that are often centuries ahead of the thinking of the later era. Even if we recall, Aristotle's genius views on slavery, we have already considered. In particular, Aristotle joined the "Liberation of Slaves" in his "wills" with the sharp changes in the production of weapons and it demanded a long time. However, this view was expressed in the existence of a slave system, and Aristotle with such an approach overtake its epoch for centuries. Shota Rustaveli's however, in epoch of the early medieval Feudalism, echoes the above mentioned opinion of Aristotle and he elevated the genius idea of freedom.[41]

The point is that Shota Rustaveli's idea about freedom of the low level was born in the 12th of century feudal Georgia (the serfdom was abolished in the 19th century) and it actually meant modernization of feudal relations. The author of genius "The Knight in Panther's Skin" ("Slave" means subordinates - "the arms") is for liberation of low class (slaves) without any conditions (contrary to Aristotle), also with a right to possess property (including gifts). We think that this idea will be strengthened by the will of Avtandil:[42]

> "I have countless possessions weighed by none: Give the treasure to the poor, free the slaves; enrich every orphan without means; they will be grateful to me, remember me, bless me; I shall be thought of."

---

[41] Silagadze, A. (2018). Some Aspects of Economic Ideas in Shota Rustaveli's "The Knight in the Panther Skin". *Bull. Georg. Natl. Acad. Sci., vol. 12, no. 1.*

[42] *The Man in the Panther's Skin* by Shota Rustaveli; Translated by Marjory Scott Wardrop [1912].P.125.

Shota Rustaveli discusses the concepts characteristic to market economy, such as: market, trade permit, buying, selling, price, profit, loss, property accumulation, etc. It is interestingly illustrating how the rules of trade operate in the town of Gulansharo (in fact, as the "International Trade Center") and the market prices there:[43]

"Tell me all in detail," quote the knight to that man; "what stuff is dearer, or what is bought up cheap?" He said, "I see, thy face seems to me like the face of the sun. Whatever I know I will tell thee truly; I will by no means inform thee crookedly."

Foreign merchants must check the merchant's elder before sales, which should also be given to a trade permit, and merchants should not be sold for a new year. Joined together:[44]

> "Great merchants can find nought more profitable than this: They buy, they sell, they gain, they lose; a poor man will be enriched in a month; from all quarters they gather merchandise; the penniless by the end of the year have money laid by."
>
> "As a rule, there was no positive attitude towards big trade in the Feudal States of that time, and there is a lot of arguments in favor of big trade in "The Knight in the Panther's Skin"[262]:
>
> "Wen great merchants can find nought more profitable than this: They buy, they sell, they gain, they lose; a poor man will be enriched in a month; from all quarters they gather merchandise; the penniless by the end of the year have money laid by."

Here, it seems that merchants from other countries are meant, who granted the most valuable items to the treasury in order to get free trade permits in the country.

In "The Knight in the Panther's Skin" free trade principle is approved - free movement of goods and protection of large traders engaged in foreign trade, because the state must establish trade rules and protect the safety of merchants. It is not accidental that one of the main heroes of "The Knight in the Panther's Skin" - Avtandil,

---

[43] Ibid, p.168.
[44] Ibid, p.168.

unselfishly helped the merchants of Baghdad to fight against the pirates. Avtandil has addressed to the caravan members:[45]

"You merchants are cowards, unskilled in war. Lest they slay you with the arrow from afar, shut the doors behind you. Behold me alone how I fight, how I use my lion-like arms;

See how I make the blood of the corsair's crew flow."

Indeed, Avtandil defeated the pirates severely in battle, and the survivors asked him to keep their life and the right to serve him:[46]

As much as his heart desired was he victorious in the fight with them. Some humbly adjured him: "Slay us not, by thy faith!" Those he slew not, he enslaved them, whoever survived his wounds. Truly saith the Apostle: "Fear makes love."

The winner of the fight with pirates Avtandil has not received a great offer of merchants. His answer is: What do I need it for? I had a lot of wealth! Be thankful to God! I will only be your companions:[47]

> "As much treasure as I desired to amass I had of mine own, countless priceless coverlets of silk. What use could I make of yours? What do I want? I am but your companion. Moreover, I have some other dangerous business."

According to Shota Rustaveli, the king must be generous and merciful especially when he has a great income; Kindness, generosity can make our enemy to be on your side; If the item (goods, property) is not used, it is worthless or inappropriate or if the property does not bring additional benefits to its ownership is worthless:[48]

> "Munificence in kings is like the aloe planted in Eden. All, even the traitor, are obedient to the generous. It is very wholesome to eat and drink, but what profits it to hoard? What thou givest away is thine; what thou keepest is lost."

---

[45] Ibid, p.168
[46] Ibid, p.165.
[47] Ibid, p.166
[48] Ibid, p.9.

Why is a coward man better to a knitter? The protection of moral norms is important when acquiring wealth:[49]

> "In what is a cowardly man better than a woman weaving a web! It is better to get glory than all goods!"

Shota Rustaveli is well aware of the charitable activities as an important and useful direction for social solidarity. Besides, it appreciates the activity, if it is carried out at the expense of its own property. In this regard, he express exemplary generosity while Tinatin's esseccion of the throne:[50]

> She sent for her faithful, trusty tutor, and said, "Bring hither all my treasure sealed by thee, all the wealth belonging to me as king's daughter." He brought it; she gave without measure, without count, untiringly.

In poem, we can consider hunting of the King the Rostovan and Avtandil - a fascinating example of good-faith-free competition. The winner must have a better result in the competition. To this end, the king ordered to tell the truth about who won over the hunt, or on the basis of the appropriate argumentation to name the winner of the competition. "The slaves" promised the king the truth:[51]

> "Together ye have slain in all a hundred score, but Avt'handil killed more by a score; he missed not even one at which he aimed his bow, but of yours we cleaned up many which left blots on the earth."

From the above mentioned it also follows that productivity, quality, accurate information, the most important element to win in free competition: the King told the truth that Avtandil won in the competition!

---

[49] Ibid, p.124.
[50] Ibid, p.10.
[51] Ibid, p.14.

A worthy person, work force is the “wealth and valuables of the country” and the purpose of the country is to create decent living conditions for a worthy person[52]

> “Avtahandil set out, a brave knight marching boldly; twenty days he journeyed, many a day he made one with the night. She is the joy of the world, she is treasure and due; he puts not away the thought of T’hinat’hin, of her for whom the flame burns”.

Even in the 12th century, Shota Rustaveli was well aware of the fact that, without labor, there was no wealth,[53] i.e., labor is one of the main factors of production:

> “Pearl falls to the lot of none without buying and bargaining.”

Consequently, the key factor for the creation of wealth, product is labour and it was long before the heated discussions on this issue would have begun in economic literature

Shota Rustaveli in his poem “The knight Panther’s Skin” used many terms with economic contents of the current period. Namely: wealth, property; Precious cloth, leather. Golden woven fabrics; War plunder, merchant; Gem; Jewelry house; Wealth, “drama” – old style silver money; Money unit; “Mint” - a weapon-making building; Goods; Profit; Fine; competition; lose; Treasury; Taxpayers; Trade; Caravans, leisure houses for merchants; Diamond processing; Doffer and, etc.

Thus, in “The Knight in the Panther’s Skin” is the genius of the economic ideas that are often precedes its epoch. Namely:

- Liberation Idea of low-class representatives from feudal regime with the right to possess property;

---

[52] Ibid, p.25.
[53] Ibid, p.27.

- Merchantilist Ideas centuries before the formation of this doctrine;
- Industry's products are of great wealth, which plays a major role both within the country and in international trade;
- Item (goods, property) without use is worthless or if the property does not bring extra income to its possession is useless;
- Opening of foreign trade markets centers is crucial for the development of foreign trade;
- He paid has less attention to the industry than the trade, but the author understands that the magnitude of trade without industrial goods can not be expanded;
- Trading and large merchants play a special role in the country and foreign economic relations, and therefore the state must protect and encourage them;
- It is necessary to determine the rules of trade, protection and preliminary study of market price conjunction;
- Foreign trade is the main source of profit and loss;
- It is important to safeguard moral standards when acquiring wealth;
- It is very importance to be free competition and to maintain its principles honestly;
- Owner of great property should be a great philanthropist;
- Charity performed only at the expense of own property is a significant direction of social solidarity;
- Work is a key factor in producing wealth and products;
- There are many economic terminology, which are still actual and so forth.

6. Albert the Great and Thomas Aquinas "Fair Price" Again

Canonists (Greek law) Ecclesiastical canonical lawmakers. The protected rules prescribed by the Church (canonical law) were preserved. In their opinion, the layers of people in society are manifestations of God's will and the function of all human beings is determined accordingly. At that time, the church strengthened its influence and became the owner of a great estate. Obviously, the canonsits were for private property.

The concept of "fair price" was founded by Aristotle and Aurelius Augustine. Tomas Aquinas (acquainted in 1245 in Paris), - the teacher of German philosopher, theologian, anchor scholar Albert von Bollstädt, Albert the Great[54] (German Albert Graf von Bollstädt) mentioned the same issue.

Albertus Magnus (Albert the Great) (1193-1280)[55] in its essay "Ethics" has established its opinions about "Fair Price". It implies the price that will cover the seller's expenses and his work. There is no benefit (interest) and profits of trade. Consequently, the well-being of the public is provided by fair exchange that will be based on the labor equivalent: If labor and other expenses (raw materials and auxiliary materials ...) Are not compensated fairly, the existing society will fall apart.

The most prominent representative of canonists is *Thomas Aquinas* (1225-1274): philosopher and theologian, ideologist of orthodox teaching, the son of the Italian Graf. He studied at the University of Naples, then in the Cologne (1248-1252) with the German theologian Albert Magnus (1193-1280).

---

[54] *Scholasticism - the theological philosophy of Europe based on the ideas of Catholicism and Aristotle.*

[55] Magnus, A. *Bishop of Ratisbon. Opera omnia*, ed. by Augustus Borgnet. 38 vols. Paris, 1890-1899.

In 1256 he became Master of the University of Paris, a year later at Sorbonne University, he received the title of Doctor. He spent the last years of his life in Italy, in 1323 he was canonized as saints.

T. Aquinas recognizes the primacy of the Church in political life, granting the monarchy dominance among the forms of governance, requiring the obedience of the king to the Church.

The system of Thomas Aquinas' view and actions in Catholic philosophy are referred to as Thomism (from the 19th century - neothomism). Thomism seeks to mix Aristotle's philosophy with Christianity. There are two directions in it: first, opponents of orthodox modernization and the second - the supporters of the "Renaissance" news.

Pope Leo XIII (1879) with an open letter, The doctrine of T. Aquinasand Thaoism declared declared as the main pillar of Catholic doctrine.

T. Aquinas, like Aristotle, felt that a person should live properly in accordance with a public interest. According to his "common well-being" concept, the problem of shared welfare is the priority compared to the individual.

T. Aquinas is the author of many works, including "Summa Theologica"[56] written in Latin language. It discusses theories of philosophy and economics.

In general, T. Aquinas like Aristotle, supports private property and makes a mistake in the opinion: more property is given to him - who has more functionality in society.

T. Aquinas also discussed the essence of the concept of "Fair Price". Moreover, he does not share: the idea of fixed price, Aristotle's approach to trade, and believes that development is impossible without trade and condemns asury (as the Bible, Aristotle and others).

[56]Aquinas, T. *The Summa Theologica* [*Sum of Theology*]. http://www. documentacatholica omnia.eu/03d/1225-1274,_Thomas_Aquinas,_Summa_ Theologiae_%5B1%5D,_EN.pdf

Specific economic views of T. Aquinas are quite diverse. In particular, in the "Summa Theologica", a wide discussion has been devoted to different aspects of the lawness-lawlessness and fraudulent problems in buying-selling, borrowing-lending processes.[57] He tried to answer the following questions:[58] how legally it is to sell something more than its value;[59] Selling defective goods is illegal or not;[60] The seller is obliged to notify the buyer about the defect of goods for sale;[61] Whether it is legal or not to sell something whole bargain more expensive than it is paid in it.[62] These issues do not lose their sensibility.

The author answers the first question as follows:[63]

- According to civil law, it is fair if the seller sells the unit expensively than its value and if the buyer buys goods at a lower price. He did not extend such an approach on cases when there is a big difference between "fair" and paid prices;
- Any violation of equilibrium between the purchase and sale of the Divine Law is illegal and the Party shall pay for it in case of significant damage. However, in this process the "slight deviation" was considered admissible;

If a person wishes to sell his goods more than just the fair price, due to the delay in payment, there is a kind of usury. Also, when the buyer wants to buy goods less than the fair price. In this case we are dealing with the borrowing signs when the buyer is given the privilege instead of paying a fair price and this is some type of usury as well. On the other hand, if the buyer wants to sell his goods less than its fair price, he

[57]Aquinas, T. *The Summa Theologica* [*Sum of Theology*] http://www.documentacatholicaomnia.eu/03d/12251274,_Thomas_Aquinas,_Summa_Theologiae_%5B1%5D,_EN.pdf

[58] Ibid, Question 77.

[59] Ibid, Question 77:1.

[60] Ibid, Question 77:2.

[61] Ibid, Question 77:3.

[62] Ibid, Question 77:4.

[63] Ibid, Question 77:1.

can not be accused in usury.[64] The opinions of the author are not clearly formed and it is difficult to understand when Buyer-seller, borrower-borrower acts naturally and when-artificially.

Depending on the foregoing: it is possible to sell goods at a higher price; The buyer can buy goods at a lower price; Great deviation from the price can not be considered as "Fair valu"; Selling goods more expensively than fair value, due to the delay in payment is a usury; When the buyer wishes to buy goods at a lower price than the fair price, in this case we are dealing with the loan signs (the buyer is given the privilege instead of paying a fair price), which is some type of usury; If the buyer wants to sell his goods less than the fair price, you can not accuse him on usury.

T. Aquinas answers the second question:[65]

- Selling defective goods is not generally inadequate if the seller does not know anything about the defect of goods. In other cases, the purchase- sale act is illegal and we deal with fraud.
- The measures to be taken at different places shall be derived from the demanded, where the abundance is, it is required to take more measures. However, in each particular place the governor must act on the basis of existing specification. Thus, the neglect of such measures is illegal, since it establishes special state institutions;
- It is not necessary the buyer and the seller to know the hidden properties of the goods, it is enough to know its general useful qualities.

Thus, the sale of defective goods is not generally illegal, if the seller knows nothing about these shortcomings; Participation of the State in

---

[64] Ibid, Question 77:2.
[65] Ibid, Question 77:2.

the delivery of goods is permissible; The buyer and the seller generally need to know the useful properties of the goods.

The author's answer to the third question:[66]

- The seller of defective goods damages the buyer if this defect threatens;
- The seller of defective goods damages the buyer if this defect threatens;
- If the sale defect is not noticeable, the buyer can not discuss it if the seller doesn't inform about it;
- It is not necessary to pre-announce the buyer about the defect of goods because the buyer will not be aware of the useful qualities of the goods (which he may be interested in) and can not compare it to other goods;
- A good seller declares the defect of goods for sale, especially if she/he realizes that the information hidden will damage the buyer;
- The deficit of goods decreases its real price.
- Thus, defective goods impose the buyer in danger; The buyer will be affected by the lack of knowledge of the goods deficit; A good seller in the trading process informs the buyer about the defect in the trading process - regardless of the expected cost reduction.
- On the fourth question - whether it is lawless to sell anything more expensive than it is paid - the author answers:[67]
- It is acceptable to exchange natural goods, as it serves to satisfy the natural demand;
- The form of exchange of commodities is unacceptable when the goods are changed for the purpose of earning money;

[66] Ibid, Question 77:3.
[67] Ibid, Question 77:4.

- Merchant is only a buyer and a seller who sells for a purpose to get a profit; Buyer is for personal use not a merchant;
- If you buy goods, improve it and sell it at a higher price, the profit earned in this case may be deemed as a labor award;
- Trade is not a illegal, but ecclesiastic figures should refrain from engaging in trade, except when they buy for personal consumption.

Thus, the purchase-sale of commodities is allowed to get income;Natural exchange of goods is acceptable, it is unacceptable to exchange goods for receiving profits; It is inconceivable for ecclesiastic figures to participate in trade, for the purpose of obtaining profit.

T. Aquinas paid considerable attention to the analysis of loan and usury issues. To this end, he tried to answer the question whether it is legitimate to issue money as a loan in order to receive the supplementary benefits.[68]

In his opinion:[69]

- Lending money is not illegal, it is permissible and advantageous;
- Lending money for the purpose of receiving benefit represents usury - it is sinful and unacceptable;
  - The lender may request return of the borrowed money (and not the additional benefit);
  - The borrower pays a usury interest on the basis of his/her own free will, as the lender won't lend the loan in any other cases.

---

[68] Ibid, Question 78.

[69] Ibid, Question 78:1.

It turns out that it is not allowed to lend money for the purpose of receiving the benefit, and without any benefit it is acceptable but such discussion is still inconsistent.

On question –If it is legitimate to sell something more expensive than it is paid in it, he answers:[70]

- The creditor can, without committing the burden of sin, by negotiating with the borrower, to receive compensation in order to give him the right to use his money. This is possible even when the borrower gets more losses without borrowing money, than a creditor;
- Anyone who has received money or other property, is not obliged to return it with a surplus because it won't be unfair. Issuing loans should be based on friendship and a wish to service. However, no one lends money with this motive;
- If the owner is participating in a trade or craftship with money or other property, he/she has a right to get benefit from the activity;
- If you mortgage your property and the creditor will use the property in exchange of the loan, the value of the use of that property should be taken into account when repayment of a loan, and if the creditor does not act so, then his action is a usury.

Conclusion

It is permissible to receive compensation from the loan voluntarily; The beneficiary, who used the property is not obliged to return the property with surplus; In the field of trade or crafts, an individual participating with his/her share is entitled to get profits derived from

[70] Ibid, Question 77:2.

this activity; The cost of utilization of property (land, house ...) Mortgaged in exchange for the loan shall be considered while paying the debt.

Overall, the attempt to create a new polytechnic doctrine based on consensus and belief compromises has met with a lot obstacles, Church has remained firmly on traditional opinions, but then upon compulsion recognized financial transactions –for purpose of receiving benefit and profit.

7. Beka and Aghbugha: The Code of Laws

As it is known, people with different professions and as well as the laws created in separate countries have contributed to the development of economics as a science. In this regard, we have already discussed "The Knight in the Panther's Skin" created in Georgia by Shota Rustaveli. This time we will consider The Code of Laws drawn up by Beka (governor of Samtskhe) and Agbugha (Beka's grandson) in Georgian historical corner (dated 13th to 14th cc).[71]

More specifically, the "Code" was intended for one of the feudal principality of Georgia (then - politically distinctive region - Samtskhe-Atabegate (Satabagoro)). Then it was a large part of the Georgian territory (Akhaltsikhe, Akhalkalaki, Artaani and Chorokhi Gorge) from Tashiskari (now Khashuri) – until Karin (now Erzurum) and the Black Sea).[72]

The "Code of Law"[73] consists of 98 articles, from which 1-65 are drawn up in the period of Beka I's governance (about 1285-1306), and 66-68 articles by Beka's grandson - Aghbugha I (14th second half). In

[71] Silagadze, A. (2017). History of Georgian Economic Thought: Relation between the Center and the Region. *Bull. Georg. Natl. Acad. Sci.*, vol. 12, no. 4.

[72] Silagadze, A., Atanelishvili, T. (2010). *Aspects of Economic Doctrines in Georgia*. San Francisco.

[73] *Code of Law by Beka and Aghbugha. Georgian Legal Monuments/Codes. I*, Collection of Low Books by Vakhtang VI, Ed. Isidore Dolidze, pp. 423-463, Tbilisi (in Georgian).

addition to the "Legal Norms" in the Code of Beka and Aghbugha, there are defined issues, such as: the property, mortgage, loan relationship, trade-finance, land rent, employment relations, etc.

From the Code it becomes clear that the farmers have free and temporary contractual relation with the landowners. The peasant's murder is evaluated at 400 Tetri, and if the farmer performed an important function for the owner, the fine was 1000 tetri.[74] Persons in capture, debt unemployment and others are named as the source of becoming a bondage. According to the feudal relations in Saatabago, the owner of the "Feud" ruled everything and the gift and possession of the land demanded obedience and loyalty.

The first part of the "Code" states:[75]

- The rule of land transfer to use and the amount of payment;
- Conditions for sale of mortgaged flat, which gave the owner the opportunity to use privileged rule for buy-out;
- The rule of the use of temporary abandoned land and if its owner appears, the land will be returned to the owner with its income (excluding expenses);
- Penalty sanctions for non-use of transferred land;
- The obligation to provide the buyer with complete information on the sale of goods (eg. horses). Otherwise, the buyer could return the goods back and claim compensation;
- In case of attack on foreign merchants and robbery of property - sanction - full compensation of the seized property and so on.

According to the second-last part of the "Code" (Aghbugha):[76]

- Borrowers of 1000 tetri have to return only 1200 tetri. In case of debt, he had to pay 5% of the principal amount together with

---

[74] Ibid, Article 11.
[75] Ibid, Article: 42-45; 53-54; 64-65.
[76] *Code of Law* by Beka and Aghbugha ...

interest. Borrower of two breads were obliged to return three units of bread to the lender.[77] In case of bread it was 50% interest, in case of money (white) - 20%. The latter is much less than the interest rate in post-Soviet Georgia in the credit over the years;

- Issues of guarantees are also governed by particular. In case of nonpayment of debt, the guarantor is also responsible. If the debtor breaks the condition, the lender has a right to make a guarantor to pay the debt. Obviously, the issuance of guarantees could be easily accessible by high-level officials by creating fewer problems;
- The employer did not have the right to treat the employee badly, but if the employee would die, the employer was responsible only for paying the rent. The use of hired labor was possible in any of the industrial activities, but the rent amount should be determined, in advance, by the contract, the contract. The possibility of recruiting workforce in the feudal era of this period and the establishment of its conditions was a clear step forward.
- The priority of trade, especially the development of foreign trade, the protection of large traders. Kill of merchants was punished with a penalty in amount of 12 thousand tetri, and of peasant - 6 thousand tetri. For seizure of the merchant's property was considered double compensation, and so forth.

On the whole, the Code of Beka and Aghbugha defined legal-economic issues of certain region and also was ahead to economic thinking of that period about mercantilism-protectionism, hired labor, loan relationships and other issues; It is a precious source for the first phase of the formation of the first doctrine of society's economic development - the priority of the formation of mercantialist-

[77] Ibid, Article: 83, 93, 65-70, 80, 96-97.

protectionist doctrine, as well as to analyze the individual elements of the market economics, to establish Doctrine for development of principles of fair and equitable development of the Center and the region.

8. Monetarism Elements: N. Orem, N. Copernicus, "Gresham's Law"

Nikolas Orem (Nicolas Oresme, 1323-1382). French philosopher, theologian, educated in Paris. He wrote on theological, mathematical and astronomical topics. It is known that his writings had a significant effect on the works of Polish Nicholaus Copernicus (Latin Nicolaus Copernicus, 1473-1543), Italian Galileo Galilei (1564-1642), French Rene Descartes (1596-1650).

N. Orem translated from Latin into French Aristotle's works: Nicomachean Ethics (1370), Politics (1374) and others. In his well-known treatise on "Origin, Essence and Circulation of Money"[78] (Approximately 1358), it is discussed: the essence of money and the history of origin,[79] money circulation and payment functions;[80] Money from gold, in deficit, etc. Cut from non-ferrous metals (silver, bronze, copper); problems of coin breaking, which will actually reduce fixed income and so on.[81]

According to N. Orem, Printing of Money should controlled by the society and not just the rulers, because they often use to print extra money and run it in circulation, and they never worry if this process stimulates inflation;[82] The power to cut coins is the state's

---

[78] Nikola Orezme. *Tractatus de Origine, Natura, Jure et Mutationibus Monetarum* [*Of the origin, behavior and changes in the law Monetarum*] https://web.archive.org/web/20080422214420/http://phare.univ-paris1.fr/textes/Oresme/Tractatus.html

[79] Ibid, Chapter 1.

[80] Ibid, Chapter 2:7

[81] Ibid, Chapter 8-11.

[82] Ibid, Chapter 12-15.

prerogative,[83] but it does not allow the inflation and the coin to be falsified, except cases: (e.g.,wars).

The monetary approaches of Orem are different from typical medieval thinking. Gold and silver are the most suitable metals that can be used on a bimetallic basis. Here the monetary ratio between metals is defined by market principles.

Overall, first attempts to justify "The Theory Metallic of Money" is shown in N. Orem's views.

8.1. Nicolaus Copernicus

In 1526,[84] the famous Polish astronomer-mathematician and economist Nicolaus Copernicus (1473-1543) in his work "On Money Printing" (1526), wrote four reasons for the disaster of the country (disorders, deaths, land infertility, and loss of the value of the coin). The fourth reason for that is the reason for the slowdown of the state: Gold is the means of exchanges, except the monetary value. In the event of loss of gold coin weight and quality, it's ability to buy on market becomes weak, which step by step is noticeable. People begin to accumulate solid money (e.g., gold). In real circulation other - less valuable metal coins are issued, which increases prices and worsens trade conditions. The deterioration may be avoided if the state refuses to establish a fixed rate on gold and will make a free exchange rate to act.[85]

N. Copernicus considered it necessary to carry out the monetary reform, which would reduce mint expenditure to a reasonable level; The real rate of coin would be determined and the quality and currency rate of the coin should not be changed without consultation with well-

---

[83] Ibid, Chapter 23.

[84] *Nicolaus Copernicus: Monetae cudendae ratio* http://www.system-polskiego-prawa-podatkowego. pl/traktat.html

[85] Ibid.

known specialists; On behalf of the state, money should be printed only one place - in the mint; After running the new money in circulation, the old one should be removed from the circulation and so on.[86]

8.2. Thomas Grasham

The monetary ideas like Copernicus were independently developed by Thomas Grasham (1519-1579).[87]

The point is that since ancient times in many countries, coins were "spoiled" with different methods and opinions, but temporarily managed to maintain its nominal value. In the end, this led to the increase in prices and the use of precious money coins as a means of accumulation. This trend was also noticed by the earliest known mercantilist Thomas Grasham. He, like Copernicus, thought that: The bad money will drive out the good money from circulation. This means that cheap money can displace expensive money from circulation, money recovered artificially by the state, eliminates artificially invaluable money, "bad" money throw outs from circulation money which is better than it in condition of fixed exchange rate and so on.

Model of "Copernicus-Grasham". Based on a similar approach to Copernicus and Grashem, it was created in the model of "Copernicus-Grasham".[88] It was formed on the basis of N. Copernicus' paper "on Money Printing" (1526) and ideas of T. Grasham (1560). (Similar opinions were expressed by N. Orem and others). According to this model, gold money will be displaced from the circulation because it has become an opportunity to accumulate money and instead of it will be used money made with other metal.

---

[86] Ibid.

[87] *Gresham's Law* by George Selgin. http://eh.net/encyclopedia/article/selgin.gresham.law

[88] IMF Working Paper. (1995). *Measurement of Co-Circulation of Currencies.* By Mr. Russell C. Krueger, Mr. Jiming. https://books.google.ge/books?id=5XvPv3vWdSQC& printsec= frontcover#v=onepage&q&f =false

Such approaches were temporarily topical when there was a gold and silver money circulation. If the value of coin was deteriorated and the nominal value would still be maintained, then the population would have been able to use the "good" money, they would have saved and collected it, but the new "bad" money with the same nominal value would be used in circulation, and the problem would continue to aggravate. Therefore, the area of action of "Copernicus-Grasham model" is temporary and valid only when the state guarantees a fixed nominal exchange rate of "good" and "bad" money, while the floating exchange rate actually determines the real "weight" of the money.

9. Ibn Haldun

The famous Arab thinker *Ibn Haldun* (1332-1406) was born in Tunisia. His parents were from Andalusia. He was also in Spain, then for a long time in Egypt (professor, judge). He died in Cairo.

Ibn Haldun is very enthusiastic with new approaches and he lawfully has the distinguished place in the history of economic thinking. He, as a scholar-historian, has given interesting economic considerations in the main work of the book of examples from the history of Arabs, Persians, Berbers and other contemporaries of the modern people "(short title "The Great History ").[89]

In the introduction to the book entitled "Muqadimmah", are presented philosophic views on the author about origin and development of the State, where economic factors have the main role.

In this work he has indicated the following stages of development:[90]

[89] *THE MUQADDIMAH Abd Ar Rahman bin Muhammed ibn Khaldun* [*Lieutenant Colonel Abdul Rahman bin Mohammed bin Khaldoun*]. Translated by Franz Rosenthal https://asadullahali.files.wordpress.com/2012/10/ibn_khaldun-al_muqaddimah. pdf

[90] Ibid, Chapter 3-15.

1. The stage of fighting for the authorities and victory. At this stage the ruler gains glory, picking taxes, protects property and ensures self-defense;
2. The stage of obtaining the full control over the population and property by the manager;
3. Rest – peace – mindedness of the royal government. At this time the scope of property ownership is expanding, the governors take care of their popularity and immortality. Attention is paid to the removal of taxes, regulation of revenues and expenditure, construction of large buildings and gifts. This is the last stage when the country is fully managed by the governor;
4. Self-satisfaction and passive Stage. When the rulers are pleased with steps made by their ancestors and live in a peaceful manner;
5. Usury and welfare stage. At this time the ruler spends a lot of accumulated wealth, solving of important state affairs is to be performed by mates, including by individuals who are not able to manage, so becomes suspicious and ruthless toward future potential heirs.

It should be noted that Ibn Haldun named economic factors as one of the main features of division of society. In particular, it considers that: the state must ensure legality (including property rights) and order protection, which encourages economic activity; The optimal taxation system, the state apparatus are important for stimulating the economy; Labor division, professional qualification improvement is an important source of economic prosperity; The aim of commercial activities is to get profit; The state should ensure a stable monetary policy that will help to maintain the money-efficiency, not to allow the artificial stimulus of the inflation (the growth of money in the circulation will be harmed by the country); The fixed price policy is dangerous and the state should not interfere with the process of price-making. It is obvious that many of his opinions are still actual.

In addition, Ibn Haldun expressed other important economic considerations:[91]

- Labor is the basis for creating material wealth. The cost of labor depends on the cost of labor and demand. Thus, we are already dealing with the novelty: labor is a factor and its cost depends on the demand and labor productivity;
- The means of existence are available in two ways: natural (horticulture, collecting, craftsmanship, trade) and unnatural (material wealth, which the governor gets due to his position);
- The price of goods depends on the cost of production, demand-supply and market conjuncture, and also on the payments;
- The state can not exist without taxes and fees;
- In order to increase revenues in the state treasury, the state should interfere with the economy (regulation of taxation, participation in domestic and foreign trade). However, if the state purchases state goods at low prices and selling it at a high price, these will create barrier for private initiatives (trade-merchants, entrepreneurs ...);
- Workers produces substantial products, which is the basis for profit in addition to the remuneration of labor i.e., profit is the value of labor. The development of civilization will be accompanied by more labor usage and therefore creation of more values (earn profit). Development of crafting also provides preparation of more luxury goods;[92]
- In the fifth chapter of the work, devoted to craftsmanship and profits, it is clear that profit is the value of human labor. Here we could clearly say that such an approach is Marxist one, if we

[91] Ibid, Chapter 5-15.

[92] Ibid, Chapter 4-11.

don't take into consideration Ibn Haldun's opinion: the profit is entirely or its large part is created by human labor. It is also said that the role of money should be performed by gold and silver coins as a measure of value and a means of accumulation.[93]

On the whole, Ibn Haldun is distinguished by the high level of economic thinking, that can be summarized as follows: Economic factors are the basis for dividing the state into stages of development; The state should ensure legitimacy and stable monetary policy; The state should take part in regulation of the economy; Labour is Depending on the requirement of labor; Labor division, professional qualification improvement, is the basis for creating an extraordinary economic wealth; The aim of commercial activities is to get profit; The state should not encourage inflation with increase of money in circulation; The money function should be fulfilled by the gold and silver coins, money has the value of the measurement and accumulating functions; the fixed price policy is dangerous for the country, the cost of goods depends on the cost of production, market conjuncture, supply and demand; The state can not exist without taxes, profit is entirely or a large part of it is created by human labor.

10. Hermolaus-Erasmus: "Pravitelnitsa"

In the end of the 15th century and the beginning of the 16th century, the era of the collapse of Russian state ended and the process of establishing a centralized state began. This is the period when large landowners - "Boyars" have begun to expand large-scale land acquisitions.

Hermolaus-Erasmus, a well-known Russian publicist who worked in the Pskov church in the 1540s, was then the priest of the church in

93 Ibid, Chapter 5-1.

Moscow. He protected the interests of the Orthodox Church and, like the canonists, gave priority to the clergy.

The socio-economic interests of local nobility from his numerous publications were the most prevalent in "Pravitelnitsa", work dedicated to the state government issues written 1540-50s ("The Goerness"). It is the first economic-political treatise in Russia that protects the feudal-linear relationships, the interests of nobility, but is against to the development of large trade and usury, also well-being of nobility on the expense of others labor.

According to Hermolaus-Erasmus's views:

- The main thing is agriculture, where wealth is created;
- The source of wealth is peasant labor;
- Labor division shall be discussed in the field of agriculture;
- It is unacceptable to accumulate wealth in a monetary form;
- It is unacceptable a product which is purchased at a low price, to be sold at a high price by a merchant and, etc.

There are mentioned two main functions of centralized state in "Pravitelnitsa": first to protect public order and second to strengthen military potential.

In addition to this, the socio-economic program of Hermolaus-Erasmus envisaged improvement of peasants' material status and for this purpose:

1. Transfer of land to peasants;
2. Peasants to pay liabilities to landholders only by 1/5 (instead of 30%) of their income and in natural form;
3. Excessive product exchange or sale of money;
4. Buying and selling of goods without any payments.

Thus, it is possible to say that "Pravitelnita" is the first Russian monument of the time where are indicated: the functions of the Russian feudal state, characteristic signs, the main field of economics, labor as a source of wealth, Economic Reform Project - Establishment of unify taxes, removing barriers to trade, importance of land distribution for farmers, negative attitude to big trade, etc.

* * *

The formation of ancient economic thinking is not a guarantee of economic development of the country. In a number of countries, economic thinking was at a higher level, they had a lot of resources, but for some reasons they did not benefit from these advantages.

Table 1. GDP per capita, billion current US dollar, 2017

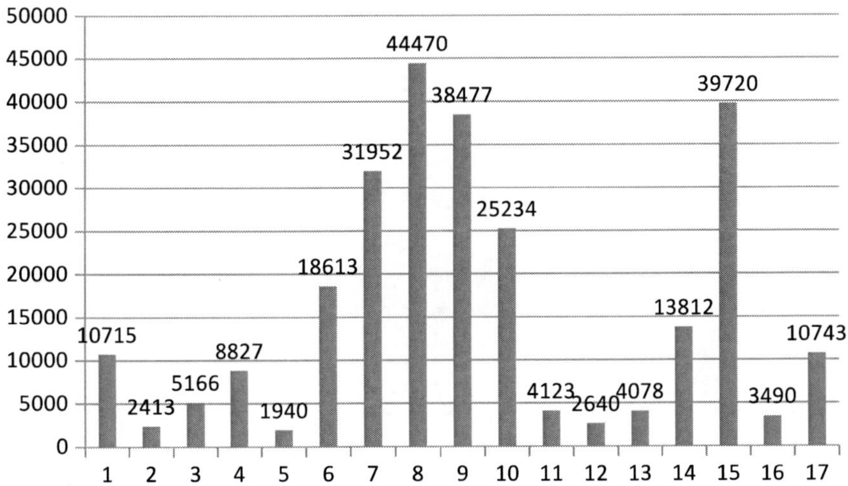

1. The world average; 2. Egypt; 3. Iraq; 4. China; 5. India; 6. Greece; 7. Italy; 8. Germany; 9. France; 10. Cyprus; 11. Algeria; 12. Ukraine; 13. Georgia; 14. Poland; 15. The United Kingdom; 16. Tunisia; 17. Russia.

(Drawn up: https://data.worldbank.org/indicator/NY.GDP.PCAP.CD 01.08.2018.)

Centuries-old development of most countries we have discussed here proves this fact. However, such a rating does not apply to all countries in the modern age: Germany, France and Italy belong to developed economies, China is the second largest producer in the world according to volume. Georgia, Ukraine and Russia are post-Soviet countries that are building more or less market economy, economy of the ancient “thinking giants”-Greek can not overcome crises, some countries have disappeared, some of them has serious problems.

To illustrate all the above-mentioned we can demonstrate the state of the countries per capita GDP to show how countries with ancient economic thinking are today according to one of the most important indicators (Table 1).

Table 1 shows that eight of the sixteen countries have average indicator; The lowest index has India, Egypt and Ukraine; The top three are Germany, the United Kingdom and France; In Greece (compared to 2008, due to crisis) and Ukraine (in recent years, domestic and Russian conflict) indicators have reduced almost 2 times.

CONCLUSION

The most important economic considerations expressed prior to economic science and doctrines' development became the basis for development of this science. Specifically what is the essence of current economic views is the following:

1. *"The instruction of Khete to Merikare"*(Egypt) came up to the forefront: the deep knowledge of state governance "rules", the role of effective operation of the management apparatus; Creating food (bread) stock Economic functions of the state; Effective management of lands; Protection of property; Youth employment problem
2. *The Code of Ur-nammu* (Shumerians) approves the military and tax reforms, lease of land, hired labor, to debt money and bread, to sell the product, terms to hire house;
3. *The laws of Eshnunna* (Iraq) were defined: Regulatory rules for trade and borrowing, means of payment for trade, shipment tariffs for ships, cash fines for human damage;
4. *"The Code of Hammurab"* (Babylon) confirms the development of commodity-money relations, existence of

ownership, lease, loan and interest rates, hire labor, forms of remuneration, money, taxes, etc.;

5. Economic thinking in China has reached a very high level of development. Here in the first millennium BC, the main field of economy was agriculture, they also produced porcelain, cannabis, paper, iron weapons, development of silk production, commodity-money thinking. These processes were reflected on Chinese economic thinking:
   (a) *Confucius* (China): condemned exploitation of local population by the state with taxes and labor relations and demanded its regulation; He distinguished collective and private property and granted the priority to the latter, he also required development of agriculture, reduction of taxes, and fair distribution of wealth.
   (b) *Mengzi* (China); Required the active interference of the state in the economy, establishment of moderate taxes, development of the goods exchange between landlords and craftsmen, the prohibition of fixed prices;
   (c) It is discussed in *Guanzi* (China): the state regulation of economy, especially the state governments of the market processes; Opportunity to determine the economic situation of the country through market and prices; Regulation of money circulation issues; Promotion of agricultural development, importance of registering the land fund; Creation of state bread stock and its distribution in the conditions of deficiency; Need for creating a special statistical institution and the use of analytical statistical materials during research; Connection between price rise and impairment of money masses; Issues of traders and men's rights limitation and protection of peasants from their exploitation, craftsmanship and trade to be deemed as the unproductive activities of the farmers; Demand for taxation in accordance with land productivity;

(d) *Laodzi* (China) condemned: unjustly accumulation of wealth, violence of the rulers and wars, causes of mass poverty - high taxes;

6. B.C. In the 6th and 5th centuries, large slave holder states were established in India, interesting written documents were drawn up:
   (a) It is developed in *The Laws of Manus* (India): the social structure of Indian community and the function of each class; the concept of "fair governance"; Regulatory norms of property relations; Workers' reimbursement forms;
   (b) *Arthashastra* (India) has been approved: Active intervention of the state in the economy, property ownership, hunger, epidemics, creating of systems that can solve problems during natural disaster, establishment of strict sanctions against barriers for human welfare, use of country's forest resources, irrigation constructions, precious metals extraction and refining, formation of warehouses, maritime communications network and strong defensive system, to legalize land ownership by peasants (tax payment), the state budget revenue-expenditure model, market conditions prior research, the state of the strict control over income and expenditures, determination of the prices of commodities according to the working days, maintenance of solid prices on the market by the state;
7. In the ancient countries, solid basis was prepared for establishment of economic science, the term "economics"was used in Ancient Greece, discusions about labor division, property and goods-money relations began:
   (a) *Xenophon* (Ancient Greece) is the first who used the term "economics", he focused on the advantages of demands and labor division, additional sources of state revenues, consumer and exchange values of goods, priority of

farming; Reimbursement of work according to the work done;

(b) According to *Plato's* (Ancient Greece) conclusion: Division of labor due to demand and natural resources conditions exchange and high productivity, together with common property, it is the basis of "ideal state" ....;

C. *Aristotle* (Ancient Greece) analyzed the most profoundly socio-economic problems of the ancient epoch and created the basis of economic science and doctrines, first used the term economic science, denied Plato's "common ownership" and privatized privileged a private property; The family (male and female), settlements were considered as the social life cell. The demand for mutual exchange has been the basis for the relationships of families and settlements; It is deemed fairly to own your private property, while it is illegal to misappropriate other's property; Disappearance of slavery is linked to the possible changes in the production of weapons, the two types of richness are distinguished: "real wealth", (economic) and "accumulation of money" (chrematistics); He explained the essence of money, the functions of the value measure, circulation and accumulation of money. Labor division, consumer value of the item and equity of the exchangeable items are named as the basis of exchange. The origin of money is connected to the inconvenience to shipments at long distances. Marine, transit and retail trade are distinguished. Has disturbed marine, transit and retail trade. He also condemns large trade and usury as a result of their risks character…;

8. According to *Epicurus* (Old Greece) each individual is able to reach prosperity without aid of the state; will be able to achieve good. *Zeno of Citium* (Cyprus) represents economics on the one hand as a practical science and divides it as moderate

(regulation of interests), regulatory (to own moderate wealth) and family economies (to achieve well-being). Stoic *Iambulus* "Greece") in his "Island of the Sun" is for existence of common property, which is actually propaganda of Plato's "communism";

9. Ancient Roman thinking of Ancient Rome is, in some ways, a peculiar continuation of ancient Greek thinking, contains nowelties adequate of time, but we think that it can not be equal to it with the depth of economic thinking. In ancient Rome, colonat was in the foreground, the introduction of new mechanisms of economy management would increase productivity. These processes were reflected in the ancient Roman economic thinking:
   (a) *Cato's* (Old Rome) Agriculture: It represents a practical guide to agriculture management of the Roman agriculture of that time, which considers the efficient management of the land (production of bread, wine and oil), and individuals working there are considered as the most hopefull workforce, the most effective force; Cato criticized large trade and usury, but still participated in this activity; According to the Cato's recommendation, the is the most effective way to produce commodity near the market, to use the hired laborers (cash or natural remuneration), development of lease relationship;
   (b) *Varro* (Old Rome) is an important contributor in the populatization process of latifundia, also in researching process of reasons for separation of farming and breeding field, in developing absolute and comparative advantages, differential rent, increasing the principles of foreign trade;
   (c) *Columella* (Rom Rome); Preferred the development of land near to the markets; development of colons, lease and commodity-money relations;

(d) *Pliny* the Elder (Old Rome) concludes that the efficient management of the land provides the abundance of harvest and reduces the price of the products, the most profitable field is viticulture and gardening near the towns, the best one is an income earned without additional expenses, the product owner must sell more products, it will provide more income without more expenditure, quality land cultivation is profitable, the market can equalize the goods, the name of the money is related to the goods, at the beginning sheep played the function of money, then bull made the same, Latifundia restricted the development of Italy and its provinces;

10. According to the concept of "Natural Right", public norms due to their natural basis, equally apply to all members of it. (Attempts to combine Plato and Aristotle's philosophies):
    (a) *Cicero*: He defended private property of latifundia and gombeen men and large land ownership; Does not approve usury, but does not contradict it; Recognizes the "natural equality" of people, including the difference of property and does not favor the common ownership of everything; The origin of private property is connected with heritage, wars, laws; The best source of income is providence; Approve the aristocratic Republic of Justice;
    (b) *Seneca* (Old Rome): He considered all people naturally "equal", "condemned" usury and high interest rate, protected the idea of equality between men and women (gladiators' battle was declared as unacceptable), the wealth was demed as a cause of prosperity and evil, the benefit of the wealth is connected only to its enactment;
    Trade was declared as a good source of income and recognized only the accumulative function of money;
11. *Brother Gracchius* (Old Rome) Agrarian Reform Project (totally unrealized) envisaged limitation the use of public lands

for large land users (Tiberius, People's Tribune); Gaius, elected as public tribune, in order to finish his brother's works enacted the law, which envisaged bread to be sold to the poor citizens cheaply, construction of the new roads (makes relations for small farmers easier), To involve representatives of lower class in the court, facilitate the military service to the poor (they no longer had to pay for military equipment) ... levied; The issue of the establishment of new land colonies in southern Italy was determined...

12. Peasants' rebellion headed by Spartacus strongly hit to slave holding regime, however they did not have any special economic demands;
13. According to the *Bible*: Payment is obligatory (tax benefits for the priests), the debt is subject to payment in the prescribed time; Strong caution is required to be fidepromissor. Usury and trade are permissible;
14. The Feudal economic visions of the new era has been reflected in the works and "codes" drawn up in different countries:
    (a) *Aurelius Saint Augustine* (Algeria): One of the first uses the term "Fair Price", usefulness of an item was logically named as one of the criteria for its evaluation, demand was basement of price formation, the rarity of the thing was named as a reason of continuous increase of prices, wastefulness, large trade and usury were condemned and charity was approved. Differentiation according to the property as allowed, the struggle for equalization of property was considered insufficient;
    (b) *The Salic Law* (Western Europe) established new forms of legal and economic relations - responsibilities for theft of property, non-payment of debt, for killing of human beings, the absence of court, property forms of land...;
    (c) According to the *"Instruction about homelands"* ("franks") it was states, that: "Homelands" must first satisfy the

personal requirement, the homeland governors have to ensure timely processing of lands (including vineyards), without loss of harvest, creation of high quality seed material supplies, special penalties were prepared for individuals who damaged the homeland, damages to homosexuals were penal sanctions, 1/10 of harvest was given to the churches, special attention should be paid to the care of the forest and special parks, they could sell the surplus product ...;

(d) *"Russkaya Pravda"* is the first law composed in Kievan Rus' which states that the regulation of criminal law, civil law and namely regulation of monetary-credit regulations;

(e) In *Shota Rustaveli's "The Knight in the Panther's Skin"* (Georgia) there are expressed many genius economic ideas, which often precedes its epoch. Namely: the idea of exemption of low class representatives from feudal regime with the right to own property; mercantilist ideas centuries before the formation of this doctrine; The importance craftsmenship, the unit usefulness criteria, the importance of foreign trade markets, the protection of large traders by the state, the preliminary study of the market price conjunction for trade; Foreign trade as a major source of profit or loss; Protection of moral norms in obtaining riches; Good protection of free competition principles; Encouragement of charity of the rich; Labor as an important factor in producing wealth; There are discussed many actual economic terminologies which are still actual…;

(f) *Canonists supported private property.* The concept of "fair price" was founded by Aristotle and Aurelius Augustine. The same issue was touched by Thomas Aquinas' teacher, German philosopher Albert von Ballenstedt-*Albertus Magnus.* According to her conclusion, the well-being of the public is provided by fair exchange, that will be based on the equivalent labor: If labor and other expenses (raw materials and auxiliary materials ...) Are not compensated fairly, the existing society will fall apart

(g) The main canonist Italian *Thomas Aquinas:* He supports private property, development of trade, condemns fixed prices and usury, and discusses various aspects of legality and illegality in buy-selling, borrowing-lending processes.

(h) *Beka and Aghbugha's code of laws* (Georgia) sets the following: Rules and conditions to transfer land, rules to buy out mortgaged land with preferential terms, sanctions for not using the lands transferred, obligation to provide buyer with information about commodity, sanctions for robbery of the foreign merchants, Started forward with sanctions, lending rates within 20% ...;

(i) The elements of the monetarism were also identified in considerations of *N. Orem* (France), *Copernicus and T. Grasham.* According to Orem (France), gold and silver should be used in exchange process with biometric basis (monetary ratio between metals should be determined by market principle), printing money should be controlled by the society and not only the rulers, the power to cut coins is the state's prerogative that should not allow the coin falsification and inflation except cases (e.g., Wars) cases; According to N. Copernicus (Poland), in addition to monetary value, gold has a function of exchange in payment, in the event of the loss gold coin's mass and quality, its purchasing power in the market weakens and begins to accumulate solid money (e.g., gold); In real circulation, the output of other low-cost metal money increases the prices and worsens the trade conditions, that can be avoided by denying the fixed currency rate of gold and activating the free exchange rate; According to

Gresham (England), under the fixed exchange rate, "bad" money crowds out of circulation better money and, etc.

(j) According to *Ibn Haldun* (Tunisia): The basis for dividing the state into development stages are economic factors; The state should take part in regulation of the economy; Labor is depended on demand; Labor division, professional qualification improvement, is the basis for creating an economic wealth; The aim of commercial activities is to get profit; The state should not encourage inflation in circulation by increasing the amount of money; The function of money should be fulfilled by the gold and silver coins, money has the value measurement and accumulation functions; Fixed price policy is dangerous for the country; The price of goods depends on production cost, market conjuncture, demand-supply; The state can not exist without taxes, the profit is entirely or a large part of it is created by human labor;

(k) *Hermolaus-Erasmus "Pravitelnitsa"* is the first Russian monument of the time that is devoted to: Functions of the Russian feudal state, characteristic signs, the main field of economy, labor as a source of wealth, surplace products, as a commodity; Economic reform project - establishment of single taxes, removing barriers to trade, importance of land distribution for farmers, negative attitude to large trade, etc.

15. The formation of ancient economic thinking is not a guarantee of economic development of the country. In a number of countries, economic thinking was at the higher level, they had a lot of resources, but for some reasons they did not benefit from these advantages.

REFERENCES

Ananiashvili, I., Achelashvili, K, Papava, V., Silagadze, A Tsereteli,G (2003). Macroeconomic regulation methods and models. *Science*, Tbilisi (in Georgian).

Ananiashvili, I., Papava, V., (2014*). Lafer-Keynesian Synthesis and Macroeconomic Equilibrium*. N.Y. Novinka.

Anchabadze, G (2005). *History of Georgia. Short sketch.* Tbilisi: Caucasian House.

Aquina, Thomas. *The Summa Theologica*. http://www. documenta catholicaomnia.eu/03d/1225-1274, _Thomas_Aquinas,_ Summa_ Theologiae_%5B1%5D,_EN.pdf.

Aristotle (1981). *Rhetoric*. Tbilisi. (In Georgian).

Aristotle. Politics. Part. 1-2. Tbilisi, 1995-1996. Tbilisi (In Georgian).

Aristotle. (2003*). Nicomachean Ethics.* Tbilisi (In Georgian).

Atanelishvili, T., Chikviladze, M, Silagadze, N. (2017). About State Financial Control, *Ecoforum Journal* 6 (1).

Atanelishvili, T., Silagadze, A. (2018). Formation of Economic Views in the Ancient Era. *Bull. Georg. Natl. Acad. Sci.*, vol. 12, no. 2.

Atanelishvili, T., Silagadze, A. (2018). Xenophon: Economy Finds Its Name. *Bull. Georg. Natl. Acad. Sci*., vol. 12, no. 4.

Atanelishvili, T., Silagadze, N. (2016). Evolutionary Aspects of the Georgian Banking System. *Ecoforum Journal* 5 (2).

Avtonomov,V., et al. (2002). *Istoriya Economicheskich Uchenii* [*History of Economics Doctrines*]. Moskow. (In Russian).

Basilia, T., Silagadze, A., Chikvaidze, T. (2001). Post-Socialistic Transformation: Georgian Economy at the Threshold of XXI Century. *"Aradani"*, Tbilisi.

Blaug, Mark (1997). *Economic theory in retrospect*. (5th ed.). Cambridge New York: Cambridge University Press.

Boatwright, Mary T., Gargola, Daniel J., Lenski, Noel,Talbert, Richard J. A. (2011). *The Romans: From Village to Empire: A History of Rome from Earliest Times to the End of the Western Empire*. Second Edition.

Cato Marcus Porcius, *Zemlodelie* [*On Agriculture*]. http://penelope.Uchicago.edu/Thayer/E/Roman/Texts/Cato/De_Agricultura/A*.html.

Cato, Varro, Columella, Pliny. (1957). *O Selskom khozaistve*. [*About agriculture*]. Moscow. (In Russian).

Chantladze, V. (1992). *Shota Rustaveli's Economic Attitudes*. Tbilisi. (In Georgian).

China: *Five Thousand Years of History and Civilization*. City University of Hong Kong Press, 2007.

Chumburidze, M (2009). *History of Economic Doctrines*. Tbilisi (in Georgian).

Cicero: O Strasti. O Druzbe. Ob obyazannostiax. [*Cicero: About passion. About friendship. About duties*.] M., 1974.

Claus, W. (2002). *Der Kodex Urnamma (CU): Versuch einer Rekonstruktion* [*The Code Urnamma (CU): Attempt to Reconstruct*].

Code of Hammurabi. (1934). Tbilisi (in Georgian).

Code of Hammurabi. https://web.archive. org/web/ 200709 212 053 29/http://www.Common law. Com/Hammurabi.html 24/08/2018.

Code of Law by Beka and Aghbougha. *Georgian Legal Monuments/Codes. I, Collection of Low Books* by Vakhtang VI, Ed. Dolidze, I. pp. 423-463, Tbilisi (In Georgian).

Columella: *Extant Works*. http://penelope.uchicago.edu/Thayer/E/Roman/Texts/Columella /de_Re_Rustica/Praefatio*.html.

Complete Works of Saint Augustine, http://www.augustinus.it/links/inglese/opere.htm.

Copernicus, N.: *Monetae cudendae ratio* [*Money to coin system*] http://www.system-polskiego-prawa-podatkowego.pl/traktat.html.

Cyropadia. *The Education of Curus By Xenophon*. Translated By Henry Graham Dakyns.

Dialogi, O Gosudarstve. O zakonax. [*Dialogues, About the State. About laws*] . M., 1965. (In Russian).

Eric Roll. (1992). *The History of Economic Thought*. (5th Ed.). London.

Gaganidze, G., (2018) Foreign Trade of Georgia, Moldova and Ukraine with the EU after signing the Association Agreement. *Ecoforum Journal*, 7, Issue 1(14).

Gresham's Law by George Selgin http://eh.net/encyclopedia/article/selgin.gresham.law.

Guanzi. Chinese text with matching English vocabulary. http://chinesenotes.com/guanzi.html.

Hermolaus-Erasmus, *"Pravitelnitsa"* [*Governor*]. http://old-ru.ru/07-45.html (In Russian).

Hunt, E. K., Lautzenheiser, M. (2011). *History of Economic Thought, 3rd Edition: A Critical Perspective*. Sharpe, N.Y.

Iadgarov, I. S. (2014). *History of economic doctrines*. Professor. Under the editorship of A. Silagadze. Tbilisi (in Georgian).

Kautilya, S., *Arthashastra* [*Economics*]. Translated into English by R. Shamasastry. https://archive.org/stream/ ArthasastraEnglish_Translation/Arthashastra_of_Chanakya-English, page/n7/mode/2 up.

Kharaishvili, E, Erkomaishvili, G, Chavleishvili, M (2015). Problems faced by the agricultural sector and agribusiness development strategy in Georgia, International Science Index 107. *International Journal of Social, Behavioral, Educational, Economic and Management Engineering*, 9 (11).

Kharitonashvili, J (1997). *Retrospective of Economic Doctrines and Modern Problems. Book 1*. Tbilisi (in Georgian).

Kiknadze, Z., *Antique Era*. https://www.nbg.gov.ge/uploads/ leqsikoni.pdf.

Kurz, Heinz D. (2013). *Geschichte des ökonomischen Denkens* [*History of economic thinking*]. München.

Laozi (1990). *Tao Te ching*. Tbilisi (In Georgian).

Laryryonok, R. *Nasledie Agragrnogo Zakona Tiberiy Grakxa: Zemelni Vopros I Politicheskaya Borba V Rime 20-X Gg. II V. Do N. E.* [*The Legacy of the Agrarian Law of Tiberius Gracchus: A Land Question and Political Struggle In Rome, the 20th Gg. II B. To N. E*] http://www.rumvi.com/products/ebook/наследие-аграрного-закона-тиберия-гракха-земельный-вопрос-и-политическая-борьба-в-риме-20-х-гг-ii-в-/f4443ebb-896b-423a-9a37-22cdf561422e/preview/preview. Html. (In Russian).

Laws of Bilalama. https://web.archive.org/web/ 20090402214542 /http://hworld.by.ru/ text/bab/bilalaw.html 24/08/2018.

Laws of the First Council of Nicaes. http://library.church.ge/ index.php? option=com_content&view=article&id=147%3A-i-&catid=34%3A 2009-12-29-11-31-8&Itemid =59&lang=ka.

Liber Historiae Francorum [*French historical*]. http://www. vostlit.info/Texts/rus/ Gesta_Fr/frametext.htm.

Lomouri, N. (1963). *Spartacus Life of Famous People*. Tbilisi (in Georgian).

Magnus, Albertus (1890-1899). *Bishop of Ratisbon. Opera omnia*, ed. by Augustus Borgnet. 38 vols. Paris.

Mark Porcius Cato. *Agriculture*. Latin text and translation http://penelope.uchicago.edu/Thayer/E/Roman/Texts/Cato/De_ Agricultura/home.html.

Mashkin, N. A. (1949). *Principat Avgusta*. [*Principate of Augustus*]. Moscow. (In Russian).

Mayburd, E. M. (1996). *Vvedenie v Istoriu Ekonomicheskoi misli*. [*Introduction to the history of economic thought*]. Moscow. (In Russian).

Mekvabishvili, E., Atanelishvili, T. (2017). Globalization: emigration and transformation. *Ecoforum Journal*, 6, 2.

Mekvabishvili, E., Atanelishvili, T. (2017). Personal remittances in post-Soviet countries (comparative analysis). *Bull. Georg. Acad. Sci.*, 11, 3.

Mengzi. Chinese text with Legge's English translation. https://ctext.org/mengzi.

Metreveli, R. (1972). *Essays from the History of Feudal Georgia*. Tbilisi (In Georgian).

Metreveli, R. (1973). *Class struggle in feudal Georgia, (XIII saukune)*. Tbilisi (in Georgian).

Metreveli, R. (1991). *Queen Tamar: Polotical, cultural and social-economic review of the epoch*. Tbilisi (in Georgian).

Mirovay Economicheskaya Misl. [*World Economic Thought*]. T.1. Moscow, 2004. (In Russian).

Moral Letters to Lucilius: Vol.1-1917; Vol. 2 – 1920; Vol. 3 – 1925.

Natadze, N. (1973). *Philosophy of Thomas Aquinas*. Tbilisi (in Georgian).

On Revenues Xenophon Translation by H. G. Dakyns. http://www.hkshp.org/wclassic/xenophon-revenues.htm.

Oresme, N. *Tractatus de Origine, Natura, Jure et Mutationibus Monetarum* [*Of the origin, behavior and changes in the law Monetarum*] https:web.archive.org/web/20080422214420/; http://phare.univ-paris1.fr/textes/Oresmee/Tractatus. html.

Papava, V. (2002). "Necroeconomics - the Theory of Post-Communist Transformation of an Economy." *International Journal of Social Economics*, Vol. 29, No. 9-10.

Papava, V. (2005). "On the Theory of Post-Communist Economic Transition to Market." *International Journal of Social Economics*, Vol. 32, No. 1/2.

Papava, V., (2009). "Post-Communist Capitalism and the Modern World of Dead Economy." *Bulletin of the Georgian National Academy of Sciences*, Vol. 3, No. 2.

Papava, V., (2010). The Economic Development Complex in the Black Sea Area: The Impact of the Global Financial and Economic Crisis. *Xenophon Paper*, No. 9, <http://icbss.org/media/113_original.pdf>.

Papava, V., (2017). "Retroeconomics – Moving from Dying to Brisk Economy." *Journal of Reviews on Global Economics*, Vol. 6, <http://www.lifescienceglobal.com/independent-journals/ journal-of-reviews-on-global-economics/volume-6/85-abstract/ jrge/2929-abstract-retroeconomics-moving-from-dying-to-brisk-economy>.

Plato (2003). *Republic*. Translated from olf Greece by Bachana Bregvadze. Tbilisi ''Nekeri'' (in Georgian).

Plato Biography, file:///C:/Users/user/Downloads/plato-257.pdf.

Plato. *Laws*. http://www.perseus.tufts.edu/hopper/text?doc=Perseus: text: 1999.01.0166.

Pliny the Elder, *The Natural History*, John Bostock, Ed. http://perseus.tufts.edu/hopper/text?doc=Perseus%3Atext%3A1999. 02.0137&redirect=true.

Plutarch (1975). *Favorite Biographies*, Tbilisi (In Georgian).

Plutarch, *The Parallel Lives. The Life of Crassus*, 8. http://penelope.uchicago.edu/Thayer/E/Roman/Texts/Plutarch/Lives /Crassus*.html.

Plutarch. *The Parallel Lives. The Life of Cato the Elder*, http://penelope.uchicago.edu/Thayer/E/Roman/Texts/Plutarch/Lives /Cato_Major*.html.

Reuven, Yaron (1988). *The laws of Eshnunna*, Brill. Second Revised Edition.

Revised By F. M. Stawell https://www.gutenberg.org/ files/2085/2085-h/2085-h.ht#2H4 0011.

Reynolds, Susan (1996). *Fiefs and Vassals: The Medieval Evidence Reinterpreted.*

Robins, Lionel (2000). *A History of Economic Thought: The LSE Lectures*. Edited by Steven G. Medema and Warren J. Samuels Princeton University Press.

Roselaar, S. (2010). *Public Land in the Roman Republic: A Social and Economic History of Ager Publicus in Italy, 396–89 BC*. Oxford: Oxford University Press.

Russkaya Pravda. [*Russian Truth*] http://www.hrono.info/dokum/1000dok/pravda72.php. (In Russian).

Salicheskaya Pravda [*Salic Truth*]. (1950). Per. N.P. Grazianovskogo. Moscow. (In Russian).

Sandmo, Agnar (2011). *Economics Evolving: A History of Economic Thought*. Oslo/by Princeton University Press.

Schumpeter, J. (2004). *Istoriya Economicheskogo Analiza*. [*History of Economic Analysis*]. T.1. St.- Petersburg. (In Russian).

Seneca, L. A. (1893). *Izbr. Pisma* [*Fav. Letters*]. SPB. (In Russian).

Shota Rustaveli (1996). *The Knight in the Panter's Skin*. Tbilisi (in Georgian).

Silagadze, A. (1991). *Economic conception of slave-holding society*. Tbilisi (In Georgian).

Silagadze, A. (1996). *Some Aspects of the History of Economic Thought*. Tbilisi (in Georgian).

Silagadze, A. (2001). *Issues of Economic Opinion History*. Tbilisi University Press. Tbilisi (in Georgian).

Silagadze, A. (2006). *Sources of Economic Doctrines*. Publication of Tbilisi University, Tbilisi (In Georgian).

Silagadze, A. (2007). *Economic Doctrine of the middle Ages*. Publication of Tbilisi University. Tbilisi (In Georgian).

Silagadze, A. (2010). Economic Thought in Feudal Georgia. *The Caucasus & Globalization*. 4, 3- 4:57–66. CA & CC Press, Sweden.

Silagadze, A. (2013). *Post-Soviet Economy: Aspects of the Georgian Economy*. http://georgiamonitor.org/.

Silagadze, A. (2013). Priorities for the Economy of Postcommunist Georgia in the Context of the World Financial Crisis. *J. Problems of Economic Transition* (USA). 56, 8: 3–16.

Silagadze, A. (2013). Some of the external aspects of the Georgian economy in modern times. *Moldavian Journal of International Law and International Relations*, 4 (30): 143-149.

Silagadze, A. (2015). Failure of the Keynesian Multiplier Doctrine: some aspects of interrelation between Investments and employment. *Topical Problems of Sustainable Development of National Economies*. TSU, Paata Gugushvili Institute of Economics. Tbilisi.

Silagadze, A. (2016). Concerning "Paradox" of Investment and Employment. In: *Innovative economics and the problems of its formation in the post-communist countries*. TSU, Paata Gugushvili Economic Institute Press. Tbilisi.

Silagadze, A. (2016). Historical Parallels of the National Economic Doctrines. Refereed *International J. Ecoforum*. 5, 2. http://www.ecoforumjournal.ro.

Silagadze, A. (2017). About Regional Economic Thought. *Ecoforum Journal*. 5, 2. 7.

Silagadze, A. (2017). From the History of Georgian Economic Thinking: structural and innovative problems of economic development. *Proceedings of Materials of International Scientific Conference Dedicated to the 65th birth anniversary of Professor George Tsereteli*.

Silagadze, A. (2017). History of Georgian economic thought: Relation between the center and the Region. *Bull. Georg. Natl. Acad. Sci.*, 11, 4.

Silagadze, A. (2017). Post-Soviet "Paradoxes" of Unemployment Rate. *Bull. Georg. Natl. Acad. Sci.*, 11, 1.

Silagadze, A. (2018). From the History of Agrarian Thought. *Journal Annals of Agrarian Science*. Elsevier. 2018/4/22.

Silagadze, A. (2018). Gini Index – Wealth Distribution in the Post-Soviet Countries. *Bull. Georg. Natl. Acad. Sci.*, 12, 3.

Silagadze, A. (2018). Some Aspects of Economic Ideas in Shota Rustaveli's "The Knight in the Panther's Skin". *Bull. Georg. Natl. Acad. Sci.*, 12.

Silagadze, A., Atanelishvili T. (2007). *Mercantilist Economic Doctrine*. Tbilisi.

Silagadze, A., Atanelishvili, T. (2010). *Modern State Finances of Georgia*. Peninsula University of Technology, Business and Informatics. San Francisco.

Silagadze, A., Atanelishvili, T. (2010). *Nekotorie Voprosi Economicheskix Dokrin v Gruzii.* [*Some Issues of Economic Doctrines in Georgia*]. Moscow. (In Russian).

Silagadze, A., Atanelishvili, T., Goshadze, G., Demetrashvili, T., Zurabishvili, V. (2005). *Comp., Encyclopedic Dictionary of Economics*. Tbilisi.

Silagadze, A., Atanelishvili, T., Silagadze, N. (2010). *Economic Doctrines*. Georgian National Academy of Sciences. Tbilisi, "Inovacia".

Silagadze, A., Atanelishvili,T., Silagadze, N. (2018). *Economic Science Origins*. Tbilisi University Press., Tbilisi. (in Georgian).

Silagadze, A., Beridze, T. (1996). Note on Privatization in Georgia. *Economic Transition in Russia and the New States of Eurasia* 8, 354-356. New York, ME Sharpe.

Silagadze, A., Gelashvili, S. (2009). *Gegenwärtige Finanzlage und Monetäre Aspekte in Georgien* [*Current Financial Position and Monetary Aspects in Georgia*]. No. G-10. Universität Potsdam.

Silagadze, A., Tanelishvili, T. (2010). *Aspects of Economic Doctrines in Georgia*. Peninsula University of Technology, Business and Informatics. San Francisco.

Silagadze, A., Tokmazishvili, M. (2009). *Challenges of the Post-communist Financial-currency Policy*. Nova Science Pub Incorporated. New York.

Silagadze, A., Tokmazishvili, M., Atanelishvili, T. (2014). Post-Communist Economic Development: Obstacles and Prospects

(A Georgian case-study). *J. The Caucasus & Globalization*. 7, 3-4: 72-81. CA&CC Press, Sweden.

Silagadze, A., Zubiashvili, T. (2015). Parameters of the European Union and the Post-Soviet Georgia's Economy. Refereed *International Journal of Business and Management Studies (IJBMS)*, pp. 441–448.

Silagadze, A., Zubiashvili, T. (2016). Foreign Direct Investment in Georgia. *Inter. Jour. of Arts and Science*. 9, 2: 63-72. (USA). http://universitypublications. net/ijas/0902/pdf/H6V7.pdf.

Silagadze, A., Zubiashvili, T. (2016). Georgia's Economy Against the Background of the Associate Agreement with the European Union. *Inter. J. of Business and Management Studies*, 59, 2: 533-540. (USA)http://universitypublications.net/ijbmsи/0502/pdf/V6Z43.pdf.

Silagadze, A. S., Sidorov, V. A., Iadgarov, I. S. (2016). *Fenomen Rinochnogo Xozaistva: Fundametalnie I Prikladnie Osnovi*. [*Market Economy Phenomenon: Fundamental and Applied Foundations*]. Tbilisi: Edition "Universali". (In Russian).

Steven G. Medema (Editor), Warren J. Samuels (Editor). (2013). *The History of Economic Thought*. Second edition Published 2013 by Routledge.

The Analects. Sayings of Confucius. Translated By D. C. Lau. https://antilogicalism.files.wordpress.com/2017/07/the-analects. pdf

The Capitulare de Villis. https://www.le.ac.uk/hi/polyptyques/ capitulare/ trans.html.

The Code of Hammurabi. Translated by L. W. King http://www. general-intelligence.com/library/hr.

The Economist by Xenophon. Translation by H. G. Dakyns. http://www.gutenberg.org/files/1173/1173-h/1173-h.htm.

The Instruction of Merikare. http://www.reshafim.org.il/ad/egypt/ merikare_papyrus.htm.

The Laws of Manus. Translation by G. Bühler. Oxford. At the Clarendon Press. 1886. https://ia800501. us.archive.org/28/items/ lawsofman00manu/lawsofman00manu.pdf.

The Man in the Panther's Skin by Shota Rustaveli; Translated by Marjory Scott Wardrop [1912]. http://www.sacred-texts.com/asia/mps/index.htm.

The Muqaddimah Abd Ar Rahman bin Muhammed ibn Khaldun. [*Lieutenant Colonel Abdul Rahman bin Mohammed bin Khaldoun*] Translated by Franz Rosenthal https://asadullahali.files.wordpress.com/2012/10/ibn_khaldun-al_ muqaddimah.pdf.

The Salic law. http://avalon.law.yale.edu/medieval/salic.asp.

Tukhashvili, M (2018). Retrospective Comprehension of Post-Soviet Georgia's Population Migration. *Bull. Georg. Natl. Acad. Sci.*, 6, 2: 175-182.

Tvalchrelidze, A., Silagadze, A. (2012) Capitalization of Mineral Commodities-World and Georgian Experiences. *Bull. Georg. Natl. Acad. Sci.*, 6, 2.

Tvalchrelidze, A., Silagadze, A. (2013). The macroeconomic model for oil exporter countries. *J. Central Asia and the Caucasus*, 16, Issue 4: 118–144, Sweden.

Tvalchrelidze, A., Silagadze, A., Keshelashvili, G., Gegia, D. (2011). *Georgia's Social Economic Development Program. "Nekeri"*, Tbilisi. file:///C:/Users/admin/Downloads/Georgia% 20social%20 economic%20 development%20program.pdf.

Tvlli M. Cicero. Dialogi. *De re publica* [*To publish*]; De Legibvs Oxford University Press, (1966). file:////Users/user/Downloads/Preview_Cicero, _J.G.F.Powell_ed._M._Tulli_Ciceronis_De_Re_Publica, _De_Legibus,_Cato_Maior_de_Senectute,_Laelius_de_Amicitia.pdf.

Varro Marcus Terentius on Agriculture. http://penelope.uchicago.edu/Thayer/E/Roman/Texts/Varro/de_Re_Rustica/1*.html#note36

Varro (1963). Selskoe Xoziaistvo. [Agriculture]. Moscow. (In Russian).

Winston, D (1976). Iambulus' Islands of the Sun and Hellenistic Literary Utopias. *Science Fiction Studies*, №10 = Vol. 3, Part 3/11.

Xenophon: *Kiropedia* [*Cyropadia*] M., 1976; *Sokraticheskoe Sochinenie*. [*Socratic writings*]; http://ancientrome.ru/antlitr/t.htm?a=1348100002; Domostroi [Oikonomikos] . M. 1993.

Zenon iz Kitiya.O Prirode. Perevod S. Arevshatyan. (1956). [*Zeno from Kitia. About nature*]. Translation by S. Arevshatyan (1956). http://www.matenadaran.am/ftp/data/Banber3/19.S.Arevshatyan.pdf. (In Russian).

Zubiashvili, T., Chikviladze, M, Silagadze, N. (2018). Some Aspects of State External Debt. *Ecoforum Journal* 7 (2).

Zubiashvili, T., Silagadze, L. (2016). Some aspects of the Georgian Economy at the contemporary stage. *Ecoforum Journal*. 5, 2.

About the Authors

Professor Avtandil Silagadze

Professor, Ivane Javakhishvili: Tbilisi State University, Faculty of Economics and Business, Chair of the Department of International Economics and Economic History, Doctor of Economic Sciences, Academician of theGeorgian National Academy of Science, Laureate of the Georgian State Prize in Science and Technology. He has published many books, articles in Georgia and abroad in Georgian, English, German, Russian and other languages. His is publications include: *Challenges of the Post-Communist Financial-Currency Policy*. Nova Science Publishers, Inc. (New York) (C./A.: 1),(2009); "Gini Index – Wealth Distribution in the Post-Soviet Countries." *Bull. Georg. Natl.*

Acad. Sci., 12, 3. (2018); “Post-Soviet ‘Paradoxes’ of Unemployment Rate.” *Bull. Georg. Natl. Acad. Sci.*, 11, 1. (2017); “Georgia’s Economy against the Background of the Associate Agreement with the European Union.” *International Journal of Business and Management Studies*. Vol. 5. №2, (C./A.: 1), (2016); “Historical Parallels of the National Economic Doctrines.” Refereed *International Journal Eco Forum*. Vol. 5. №2. (2016); “Foreign Direct Investment in Georgia.” *International Journal of Arts & Sciences* 9 (2), 63 (2016) and others.

Email: avtandil.silagadze@tsu.ge

Dr. Tamar Atanelishvili

Dr. Tamar Atanelishvili: Associate Professor of the Faculty of Economics and Business, Ivane Javakhishvili Tbilisi State University, Doctor of Economics. Publications include: “Formation of economic views in the ancient era.” *Bull. Georg. Natl. Acad. Sci.* 2 (1), (2018); “Globalization: Emigration and Transactions.” *Ecoforum Journal* 6 (2), (C./A.: 1), (2017); “Some Aspects of National Economic Doctrine.” *Ecoforum Journal* 6 (1), (C./A.: 1), (2017); “Personal Remittances in the Post-Soviet Countries (Comparative Analysis).” *Bull. Georg. Natl. Acad. Sci.* 11 (3), (C./A.: 1), (2017); “Georgian Experience in Functioning of State Statistic Body.” *Ecoforum Journal* 5 (2), (2016) and others.

Dr. Nodar Silagadze

Dr. Nodar Silagadze: Higher School Georgia, Associate Professor, Doctor of Economics and Business. Ministry of Finance of Georgia, Budget Department Senior Specialist. He is engaged in research in the field of financial and banking systems, transformational economy, international economics, economic thought history, budget planning and international financie. He passed practical seminars and training in Slovenia, Japan, the Netherlands. His is publications include: "Some Aspects of State External Debt." *Ecoforum Journal* 7 (2), (C./A.: 2), (2018); "About State Financial Control." *Ecoforum Journal* 6 (1), (C./A.: 2), (2017); "Evolutionary Aspects of the Georgian Banking System." *Ecoforum Journal* 5 (2 (C./A.: 1), (2016) and others.

INDEX OF TERMS

O

P

R

S

T

U

V

X

INDEX OF NAMES

A

B

C

Related Nova Publications

Overshooting the Maastricht Criteria: External Imbalances and Income Convergence in the European Union

Author: Menbere Workie Tiruneh, Ph.D.

Series: Economic Issues, Problems and Perspectives

Book Description: The book discusses theoretical controversies and state-of-the art empirical studies on the link between external imbalances and real income convergence in the European Union.

Hardcover ISBN: 978-1-53613-585-5
Retail Price: $160

Challenges and Opportunities for Eurozone Governance

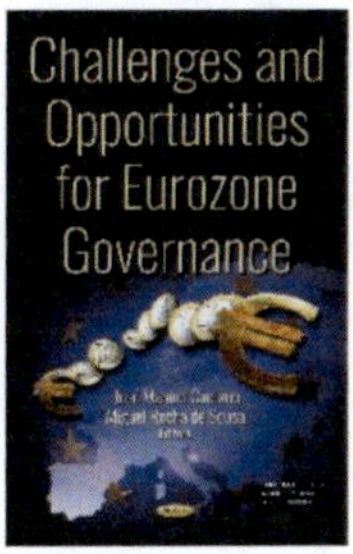

Editors: José Manuel Martins Caetano and Miguel Rocha de Sousa

Series: Economic Issues, Problems and Perspectives

Book Description: This book discusses and proposes responses to the challenges of devising viable governance, oriented to the progressive reduction and sharing of risks, in a more European oriented perspective, in which central and peripheral countries find their ways to prosperity.

Hardcover ISBN: 978-1-53613-474-2
Retail Price: $230

To see a complete list of Nova publications, please visit our website at www.novapublishers.com